RADICAL

RECONCILIATION

The Journey of

FORGIVENESS

PICKINGUP
The PIECES

by Ramon Presson with Ben Colter

Radical Reconciliation: The Journey of Forgiveness
© 2006 Serendipity House

Published by Serendipity House Publishers
Nashville, Tennessee

ISBN: 1-5749-4221-2

Dewey Decimal Classification: 179
Subject Headings: FORGIVENESS

Unless otherwise indicated, all Scripture quotations are taken from the
Holman Christian Standard Bible®,
Copyright © 1999, 2000, 2002, 2003 by Holman Bible Publishers. Used by permission.

Scriptures marked NASB are taken from the *New American Standard Bible*®,
Copyright © 1960, 1962, 1963, 1968, 1971, 1972, 1973, 1975, 1977, 1995 by the
Lockman Foundation. Used by permission. (www.lockman.org)

Scriptures marked NIV are taken from the *Holy Bible, New International Version,* Copyright
© 1973, 1978, 1984 by International Bible Society. Used by permission.

To purchase additional copies of this resource or other studies:
ORDER ONLINE at www.SerendipityHouse.com;
WRITE Serendipity House, 117 10th Avenue North, Nashville, TN 37234
FAX (615) 277-8181
PHONE (800) 525-9563

1-800-525-9563
www.SerendipityHouse.com

Printed in the United States of America
13 12 11 10 09 08 07 06   1 2 3 4 5 6 7 8 9 10

CONTENTS

Group Meeting Structure

Each of your group meetings will include a four-part agenda.

1. Breaking the Ice:

This section includes fun, uplifting questions to warm up the group and help group members get to know one another better, as they begin the journey of becoming a connected community. These questions prepare the group for meaningful discussion throughout the session.

2. Discovering the Truth:

The heart of each session is the interactive Bible study time. The goal is for the group to discover biblical truths through open, discovery questions that lead to further investigation. The emphasis in this section is two-fold: (1) to provide instruction about the process of recovery and freedom; and (2) understand what the Bible says through interaction within your group.

NOTE: To help the group experience a greater sense of community, it is important for everybody to participate in the "Discovering the Truth" and "Embracing the Truth" discussions. Even though people in a group have differing levels of biblical knowledge, it is vital that group members encourage one another share what they are observing, thinking, and feeling about the Bible passages.

3. Embracing the Truth:

All study should direct group members to action and life change. This section continues the Bible study time, but with an emphasis on leading group members toward integrating the truths they have discovered into their lives. The questions are very practical and application-focused.

4. Connecting:

One of the key goals of this study is to lead group members to grow closer to one another as the group develops a sense of community. This section focuses on further application, as well as opportunities for encouraging, supporting, and praying for one another.

Taking it Home:

Between each session, there is some homework for group members. This includes a question to take to God or a question to take to the heart, and typically a few questions to help prepare for the next session. These experiences are a critical part of your journey of forgiveness.

Radical Reconciliation:
The Journey of Forgiveness

Relationship are complex, and there are many forces at work to sabotage them. We all have busted relationships! Some are new; some are old. Some are fully inflamed; others are just simmering. Sometimes we're the offender; sometimes we're the person offended; and sometimes ... we have no clue what the problems is.

In *Radical Reconciliation*, we'll go beyond improving or managing our difficult and strained relationships. We'll pursue their healing. Our goal will be to progressively move toward forgiveness and, in most cases, healthy reconciliation. Although we're entering uncomfortable territory, bear in mind that we are on healing ground. We'll encounter some radical ideas that oppose our natural human responses. It will be important for us to remember as we continue on this journey that the work of forgiveness is a supernatural task for which supernatural power is available.

Lewis Smedes, author and noted authority on forgiveness, points out that forgiveness, which is so beyond our natural ability and instincts, is as much of a miracle as walking on the water. Forgiveness definitely sounds like a superhuman quality! For true reconciliation to occur, we need to take the path to true forgiveness, rather than settling for a cheap imitation.

Our Route to Reconciliation

Awaken: Grapple with the complexities of relationships, and the set of forces at work to disrupt and sabotage them.

Act: Understand the benefits of forgiveness and my resistance; then make a decision to take the path of forgiveness, even if it's difficult.

Analyze: Begin to push the flywheel and inch forward by analyzing relationships and naming offenses.

Release: Release is the critical juncture at which you extend compassion and gift the offender.

Reconcile: Recognize the difference between reconciliation and restoration, readjust your heart, and then take steps to build bridges.

Rebuild: The journey to personal healing and relational reconciliation is ongoing. Continue to incorporate what you've learned through this study, what God has revealed through other channels, and the discernment that you've developed as you press on in life.

SABOTAGED RELATIONSHIPS

BREAKING THE ICE – 15 MINUTES

LEADER: Be sure to read the introductory material in the front of this book and the leader's material at the end of the book. For the first icebreaker, help your group members get to know one another by initiating introductions. You should introduce yourself first. Encourage everyone to answer the "Breaking the Ice" questions, so they get used to hearing their own voices.

1. Take turns introducing yourselves to the group. Share your name, one thing about yourself that your friends would say is unusual or unique, and finally one reason you joined the group.

2. From the list below, which is your favorite to build, create, re-model, or redecorate?

   ❏ Model airplane, ship, or car – I love to imagine what it would be like to be in one.
   ❏ Kitchen – It's my favorite room!
   ❏ Bathroom – It's nice to put my own "stamp" on this room.
   ❏ The whole house – It's my prize possession.
   ❏ Old cars – I love it when a plan comes together.
   ❏ Art – I enjoy expressing myself through my creativity.
   ❏ Garden – I love the beauty of God's creation.
   ❏ Other: _____.

3. When something is broken, my first thought is usually …

   ❏ Run and hide!
   ❏ It can wait. I'll get around to it later.
   ❏ Somebody help me PLEASE!
   ❏ Not a problem. I can fix it.
   ❏ The world has just stopped and this is all I can think about right now.
   ❏ It wasn't me!

4. Briefly describe the last time you had to deal with a major repair.

OPENING PRAYER

God, we're not exactly sure how it happened, but somehow the gift of relationship gets busted. We don't know how to put it back together. In some cases, we're not even sure we want to or that it's even possible. Please walk with us in our journey toward healing as You begin to mend the broken pieces of our relationships and our hearts.

THE ANATOMY OF BROKEN RELATIONSHIPS

Before a surgeon begins surgery, he or she must first understand how the patient is wounded or impaired. A heart surgeon, for example, studies how a healthy heart functions before he or she can restore one to its original, healthy design. We must approach healing of broken relationships in the same way a surgeon studies to heal the body. In order to move toward forgiveness, healing, and possible reconciliation, we must understand the original, healthy design of the relationship and what has been broken.

In this session we will identify God's original design for human relationships and our Adversary's attempts to destroy them.

OBJECTIVES FOR THIS SESSION:

- Discover God's original design and purpose for human relationships
- Recognize the complexities of relationships and the complications of communication
- Acknowledge the intent of the Adversary to sabotage our relationships, destroy community, and isolate us from one another
- Prepare to begin the healing journey toward forgiveness and possible reconciliation

DISCOVERING THE TRUTH – 35 MINUTES

LEADER: Explain that the "Discovering the Truth" section that provides understanding of the journey of forgiveness, and opportunities to discover what the Bible says about it. Watch your time so you can leave ample time for the "Embracing the Truth" and "Connecting" segments later in this session at the end of your group session. Read any explanations and questions to the group.

The self-help section of any bookstore is full of books that address relationship issues with bosses, co-workers, parents, children, in-laws, spouses, and ex-spouses, just to name a few. There's no shortage of experts in these areas. This is indicative of the extent of broken, or strained, relationships in our culture. They're everywhere and generally unavoidable.

In this study, we'll go beyond improving or managing our difficult and strained relationships. We'll pursue their healing. Our goal will be to progressively move toward forgiveness and, in most cases, healthy reconciliation. Although we're entering uncomfortable territory, bear in mind that we are on healing ground. We'll encounter some radical ideas that oppose our natural human responses. It will be important for us to remember as we continue on this journey that the work of forgiveness is a supernatural task for which supernatural power is available.

CREATED FOR RELATIONSHIP

The Trinity existed before the foundation of the world. Within the Trinity, the Father, the Son, and the Holy Spirit have always been in relationship with one another.

> LEADER: *Ask various members to read Bible passages when they appear during the session. Encourage individuals to respond to the questions as they feel comfortable. Some members may want to speak up while others may wish to remain quiet on certain questions. Strive for participation across the group rather than allowing one or two to carry the discussion.*

1:26 Then God said, "Let Us make man in Our image, according to Our likeness; and let them rule over the fish of the sea and over the birds of the sky and over the cattle and over all the earth and over every creeping thing that creeps on the earth." 27 God made man in His own image, in the image of God He created him; male and female He created them. ...
2:18 Then the LORD God said, "It is not good for man to be alone; I will make him helper suitable.

GENESIS 1:26-27; 2:18 NASB

1. To whom does it appear "Us" and "Our" refer in verse 26? What are some implications you can imagine of being created in the image of God, of being God's image-bearer?

2. What do you think "suitable" means? What do you think Genesis 1:27 and 2:18 reveal about God's perspective on human relationships?

In addition to man's capacity for emotion, creativity, intelligence, and moral awareness, man possesses the capacity for relationship. Part of what it means to be created in the image of God is to have this capacity for relationship. We crave relationships just as we crave intimacy. In fact, relationships are vital to spiritual health. Our relational God designed us with a longing to know and to be known. It is part of our original, healthy design—our inherent DNA.

3. If God created us for relationship, what do you think He intended our relationships to be like? Ideally, what relationship qualities would be evident?

"Now, Father, glorify Me in Your presence with that glory I had with you before the world existed."

JOHN 17:5 HCSB

"For the creation waits in eager expectation for the sons of God to be revealed. ... We know that the whole creation has been groaning as in the pains of childbirth right up to the present time."

ROMANS 8:19,22 NIV

[1] How great is the love the Father has lavished on us, that we should be called children of God! And that is what we are! The reason the world does not know us is that it did not know him. [2] Dear friends, now we are children of God, and what we will be has not yet been made known. But we know that when he appears, we shall be like him, for we shall see him as he is. [3] Everyone who has this hope in him purifies himself, just as he is pure.

1 JOHN 3:1-3 NIV

4. In John 17:5, Jesus recalls the transition in His relationship with the Father. How does He seem to feel about this change? What is Jesus' desire?

5. We were originally created for deep, intimate relationship we God. Although we've fallen from this depth of relationship, what awaits us according to I John 3:1-3 and Romans 8:19?

The Trinity longs to return to that state of original relationship, and to draw us into this relationship. All of creation longs for this same return to oneness with our Creator. Because we're created in God's image, when relationships are less than what they should be, we experience a longing that requires healing and reconnection.

SUBTLE SABOTAGE IN RELATIONSHIPS

Social scientists accurately view our relationships as part of a vast and very dynamic network of contributors and influencers. They typically identify three major players in the in the network, but unfortunately they miss the fourth. This often forgotten character is our adversary, who would choose to remain anonymous and faceless because his potential damage is greatest when he's allowed to work behind the scenes.

God

Myself   Others

obvious & familiar

---

subtle & hidden

The Adversary

[10] Be strengthened by the Lord and by His vast strength. [11] Put on the full armor of God so that you can stand against the tactics of the Devil. [12] For our battle is not against flesh and blood, but against the rulers, against the authorities, against the world powers of this darkness, against the spiritual forces of evil in the heavens.

EPHESIANS 6:10-12 HCSB

Be sober! Be on the alert! Your adversary, the Devil, is prowling around like a roaring lion, looking for anyone he can devour.

1 PETER 5:8 HCSB

6. Who is our unseen adversary and what does he intend for our lives and relationships according to Ephesians 6:10-12 and 1 Peter 5:8?

The Bible makes it clear that the Devil and his demons are ruthless and purposeful. They desire to thwart and undermine everything godly. The enemy strategically schemes to sabotage lives and ruin relationships. In so doing, he seeks to diminish our capacity to bring glory to God and live in the joy God has planned for us. Although there are many factors that influence our relationships, our adversary has used four primary tactics from the beginning.

Tactic 1: Deception

LEADER: *Invite 3 people to read the parts of the narrator, the serpent/adversary, and Eve.*

NARRATOR: [1] *Now the serpent was the most cunning of all the wild animals that the LORD God had made. He said to the woman,*

ADVERSARY: *"Did God really say, 'You can't eat from any tree in the garden'?"*

EVE: [2] *"We may eat the fruit from the trees in the garden. [3] But about the fruit of the tree in the middle of the garden, God said, 'You must not eat it or touch it, or you will die.'"*

ADVERSARY: [4] *"No! You will not die. [5] In fact, God knows that when you eat it your eyes will be opened and you will be like God, knowing good and evil."*

GENESIS 3: 1-5 HCSB

7. What is the progression of the adversary's deception with Eve? What is he trying to get her to doubt?

LEADER: *If possible, use a Swiss Army Knife or something similar as a visual aid while you're discussing this section.*

Think of deception as a Swiss Army Knife that has several options hidden in the handle. These are some of the specific tools at his disposal within the main "handle" of deception:

•Temptation • Division • Destruction • Distrust • Doubt·
• Betrayal • Dishonesty • Neglect

8. Look again at the dialog. How are the various tools of deception employed in Genesis 3?

Clearly, the serpent twisted the truths that God had revealed to both Adam and Eve. The adversary came in disguise. He strategically worked to get the couple to doubt the heart of God toward them. In the deception, he took advantage of questions that were already there, and manipulated the truths to an extent that led to catastrophe.

Tactic 2: Resignation

⁶ Then the woman saw that the tree was good for food and delightful to look at, and that it was desirable for obtaining wisdom. So she took some of its fruit and ate it; she also gave some to her husband, who was with her, and he ate it.

Genesis 3:6 HCSB

9. Resignation can be understood as being passive in the path of relational destruction. In what ways to you see resignation as a force with Adam and Eve? What are your clues?

It was easy for Adam and Eve to take those first steps toward disobedience once they engaged the serpent's conversation. They allowed the serpent to dictate the terms and direction of the conversation. Once Adam and Eve resigned control, stepped aside, and listened in earnest, the story took a sudden and dramatic turn.

Tactic 3: Hiding and Secrecy

⁷ Then the eyes of both of them were opened, and they knew they were naked; so they sewed fig leaves together and made loincloths for themselves. ⁸ Then the man and his wife heard the sound of the Lord God walking in the garden at the time of the evening breeze, and they hid themselves from the Lord God among the trees of the garden. ⁹ So the Lord God called out to the man and said to him, "Where are you?" ¹⁰ And he said, "I heard You in the garden, and I was afraid because I was naked, so I hid."

Genesis 3:7-10 HCSB

10. What are some reasons you see that might have caused Adam and Eve to hide? Why would the enemy want to encourage our tendency toward hiding and secrets? Why is this so detrimental?

When we allow relationships to fall apart and accept this as a new reality, we validate one of the primary works of the enemy—resignation. This path of resignation culminates in a passiveness and shame that leaves people isolated, lonely, bitter, and vulnerable.

Tactic 4: Blame

[11] Then He [God] asked, "Who told you that you were naked? Did you eat from the tree that I had commanded you not to eat from?" [12] Then the man replied, "The woman You gave to be with me—she gave me some fruit from the tree, and I ate." [13] So the Lord God asked the woman, "What is this you have done?" And the woman said, "It was the serpent. He deceived me, and I ate."

Genesis 3:11-13 HCSB

11. What dynamic is occurring in Genesis 3:11-13? Who is each person holding responsible? Who is really to blame? How do you suppose the conversation went between Adam and Eve after they were expelled from the Garden of Eden?

Part of being human is wanting to assign blame when something goes wrong. When a relationship is injured, we want to find blame—even if it's on ourselves. When we feel deeply wounded by another, we might wonder why God didn't shield us. We tend to place the responsibility for damaged relationships with others, God, or ourselves. All three of these options are obvious and familiar and therefore the most likely targets when we look to assign blame. The enemy likes to work in the shadows. His preferred activity remains subtle and hidden.

EMBRACING THE TRUTH – 20 Minutes

> LEADER: *"Embracing the Truth" is the section in which the group members will begin to integrate the truth they are discovering during the session into their personal lives. Be aware that the level of hurt and response to this hurt will be different for different people, so the rate of life application will vary accordingly.*

Understanding the Complexity of Relationships

One of the factors that make relationships so challenging are the differences that we each bring to the table. Differences in the following categories have the potential to complicate relationships ...

Personalities	Experiences	Expectations
Educational backgrounds	Backgrounds	Ethnic Cultures
Genders	Ages	Generations
Geographic Cultures	Ambitions	Beliefs
Opinions	Convictions	Values
Priorities	Family Systems	

1. Recall a recent relationship challenge. Choose one or two of the differences noted above that complicated the relationship. What was the complication?

2. Which relationship sabotage tactic (deception, resignation/passivity, hiding/secrecy, or blame) is most prominent in this relationship? In what ways have you allowed the enemy to infiltrate?

3. Which tools from the enemy's deception toolbox (refer to page 11) are at work in this relationship?

RELATIONAL SHIELDS: RECOGNITION AND RENUNCIATION

One of the results of Garden of Eden episode is that the adversary successfully placed a wedge between Adam and Eve and God. Their relationships were never the same.

The good news is that God is not only a Creator, He is also a Healer and Redeemer. There is power in recognizing this truth. Recognition of the enemies schemes, and of the truth, act as a shield to deflect the enemy's arrows of deception and fiery arrows of shame.

4. What lies have you heard playing over and over in your mind about yourself, God, or the other person as a result of the adversary's deception? Are there any beliefs you've been carrying that just might be lies?

Territory in our personal lives and in our relationships where the enemy seems to have won can be recaptured by God. In C.S. Lewis' novel *The Lion, the Witch, and the Wardrobe*, Aslan overturns the White Witch's reign and rule over Narnia. Aslan's restored rule includes the active participation of Peter, Susan, Edmund, and Lucy. Likewise, God seeks to enlist our active participation in the restoration of our broken relationships, and the renunciation of the enemy. When it's His flag that is raised in victory on the hill of our hearts, we will join Him in the celebration. This triumphant march begins when we recognize the spiritual battle taking place against the principalities of darkness. It progresses when we renounce the Adversary's subtle influence over our hearts.

5. Rate your current level of recognition of the enemy's influence and your willingness to renounce his lies and work to reconciling relationships.

1.............2.............3.............4.............5.............6.............7.............8.............9.............10

Don't see it and
I'm not ready yet

Strong recognition, but
I'm not really ready to
renounce

Strong recognition
and I'm ready to fight

OUR ROUTE TO RECONCILIATION

On the journey to reconciliation our Route to Reconciliation will help us understand where we are in the process while keeping the destination clearly in our path.

AWAKEN: Grapple with the complexities of relationships , and the set of forces at work to disrupt and sabotage them.

ACT: Understand the benefits of forgiveness and my resistance; then make a decision to take the path of forgiveness, even if it's difficult.

ANALYZE: Begin to push the flywheel and inch forward by analyzing relationships and naming offenses.

RELEASE: Release is the critical juncture at which we extend compassion and gift the offender.

RECONCILE: Recognize the difference between reconciliation and restoration, readjust your heart, and then take steps to build bridges.

REBUILD: The journey to personal healing and relational reconciliation is ongoing. Continue to incorporate what you've learned through this study, what God has revealed through other channels, and the discernment that you've developed as you press on in life.

During the second session we will continue the process of awakening to the realities of broken relationships and healing.

CONNECTING – 20 MINUTES

Imagine that you are placing a "lost" ad in the Lost & Found section of your community newspaper. Describe your losses in a written ad, and then share your ad with the group. Here's an example of how one could read:

> Husband lost to divorce on March 4th along with capacity to trust. Also missing is peace, joy, and self-esteem. Dreams of our 20th wedding anniversary were stolen at the same time. Dreams have been replaced by nightmares and insomnia. If grip on sanity and the ability to hope again are found please return to Angela Smith, 117 10th Avenue North, Nashville, TN 37234. A reward is offered.

Discuss the following questions with your group:

1. In writing from this objective perspective, did you understand any of your story in a different light? Discuss.

2. What has been "stolen" from you?

3. The writer of the example ad hopes to recover joy, peace, and self-esteem. What do you hope to recover? What are some of the deepest longings you feel?

Let's pray for God to fill these longings in our hearts. How can we pray for you today?

MY PRAYER REQUESTS:

MY GROUP'S PRAYER REQUESTS:

LEADER: Say something like, "In today's session, we established that there is another character in the story. This character prefers to remain hidden and work in subtle ways. He wants more than anything to disrupt the harmony that God intended for us. In order to recover what we've lost, we must recognize the work of the enemy and the provisions of the Redeemer." NOTE: Be sure to give an overview of the "Taking It Home" assignment.

Taking It Home

Questions to Take to My Heart

Look into your heart for the answer to these questions. This is introspection time—time to grapple with what drives your thinking and behavior. **Every action has a corresponding belief that drives it.** Dig for what you believe in the deep recesses of your heart about God, yourself, and the world in which you live. Be sure to capture your thoughts.

✳ How have I been processing my busted relationship?

✳ To what have I attributed the cause of most of my relationship problems?

✳ To what degree have I understood the spiritual battle for the health of my relationships?

Looking Forward ... Prepare for Session 2

NOTE: Be sure to review the Group Covenant on the next page so you're prepared for a brief group discussion at the next meeting.

Consider two questions to be discussed in Session 2. Capture your thoughts and feelings in the "Relationships Journal" on page 20, as you continue on your journey.

1. Who in my life requires the most of my patience? What is it about is person, me, and the chemistry between us that makes the relationship a struggle?

2. Which of my characteristics might require others to be patient with me? Is there something I need to address here?

Group Covenant

As you begin this study, it is important that your group covenant together, agreeing to live out important group values. Once these values are agreed upon, your group will be on its way to experiencing true redemptive community. It's very important that your group discuss these values—preferably as you begin this study.

* Priority: While we are in this group, we will give the group meetings priority. All the sessions are integrated, with each session building on the sessions that precede them. Committed attendance is vital to our healing journey together.

   NOTE: Due to the focus of this group on taking the journey through the emotions and losses of divorce, group sessions will require a full 90 minutes to complete, so plan accordingly.

* Participation and Fairness: Because we are here to receive help, we commit to participation and interaction in the group. No one dominates. We will be fair to others and concentrate on telling our own stories briefly.

* Homework: Homework experiences are an integral and vital part of the recovery process. Assignments between each session include: (1) A Question to Take to My Heart or (2) A Question to Take to God; plus (3) Thoughts to journal to prepare for the next session.

* Respect and Ownership: Everyone is given the right to his or her own opinions, and all questions are encouraged and respected. We will not judge or condemn as others share their stories. We are each responsible for our own recovery and will not "own" someone else's. Offensive language is not permitted.

* Confidentiality: Anything said in our meetings is never repeated outside the meeting without permission from the group member. This is vital in creating the environment of trust and openness required to facilitate the healing and freedom. Names of attendees will not be shared with others.

* Life Change: We will regularly assess our progress and will complete the "Taking it Home" activities to reinforce what we are learning, and to better integrate those lessons into our personal journeys.

* Care and Support: Permission is given to call upon each other at any time, especially in times of crisis. The group will provide care for every member.

* Accountability and Integrity: We agree to let the members of our group hold us accountable to commitments we make in whatever loving ways we decide upon. Unsolicited advice-giving is not permitted. We will build a close relationship with an accountability partner for mutual growth and responsibility. Men will help men and women will help to women in order to uphold the spirit of integrity. No dating within the group!

* Expectations of Facilitators: This meeting is not professional therapy. We are not licensed therapists. Group facilitators are volunteers whose only desire is to encourage people in finding freedom and hope.

I agree to all of the above _____ date: _____

Relationships Journal

FORGIVENESS: WHAT IT IS. WHAT IT AIN'T.

BREAKING THE ICE – 15 MINUTES

> LEADER: *Encourage each group member to give a response to the "Breaking the Ice" questions. This gets people to join in on fun, lighter topics. If someone can't think of an answer say, "We'll come back to you." After others in the room have shared, swing back around to people you skipped.*

1. Choose a superhero from the following list. What special power, quality, or accessory does he or she have that you'd like to have? Why?

   ❏ Superman
   ❏ Batman
   ❏ Spiderman
   ❏ Wonder Woman
   ❏ Flash
   ❏ Supergirl
   ❏ The Hulk
   ❏ Mr. or Mrs. Incredible
   ❏ Other: _____

2. If you could have any special "relational power," what would it be?

3. Volunteer something about yourself that only a few people might know.

4. How did your "Taking it Home" activities go? What did you hear from your heart as you spent time dealing with causes of your relational struggle.

5. What did you learn about what you're impatient with, or how some of your personal characteristics might make others impatient?

Opening Prayer

Dear God, forgiveness feels like it will require a heroic effort on our part. We're not sure we're up to the challenge. We know we'll need Your supernatural power. Meet us here. Help us to accurately view forgiveness. We want to be drawn to it as we are drawn to a warm fire.

Objectives for this Session:

- Discover the difference between tolerance and forgiveness
- Determine our level of sensitivity
- Recognize the forgiveness imposters
- Learn how to recognize authentic forgiveness

Discovering the Truth - 35 Minutes

Mistaken Identity

"It's a bird. It's a plane. No ... it's Superman!" What do you make of a guy with a cape who's body-surfing the clouds? You can understand how people on land might have difficulty correctly identifying the red and blue blur in the sky. People frequently make flawed evaluations. "I'm sorry, officer. I thought the light was still yellow." We are uncertain about correct interpretations. "I know this is a poem, but beyond that I'm lost." In the same way, when asked to positively identify forgiveness in a line-up, we scratch our heads. Real forgiveness doesn't look like we think it should. Surely that couldn't be it.

In the "AWAKEN" step of our journey, we'll take a closer look at what forgiveness is <u>not</u>, and also examining the meaning of authentic forgiveness.

OUR ROUTE TO RECONCILIATION

AWAKEN: Grapple with the complexities of relationships, and the set of forces at work to disrupt and sabotage them.

ACT: Understand the benefits of forgiveness and my resistance; then make a decision to take the path of forgiveness, even if it's difficult.

ANALYZE: Begin to push the flywheel and inch forward by analyzing relationships and naming offenses.

RELEASE: Release is the critical juncture at which you extend compassion and gift the offender.

RECONCILE: Recognize the difference between reconciliation and restoration, readjust your heart, and then take steps to build bridges.

REBUILD: The journey to personal healing and relational reconciliation is ongoing. Continue to incorporate what you've learned through this study, what God has revealed through other channels, and the discernment that you've developed as you press on in life.

LEADER: *Read the explanations between the questions for the group. Encourage everyone to participate in responding to the questions. Ask for volunteers to read the Bible passages. Be sure to leave ample time for the "Embracing the Truth" and "Connecting" segments later in the session.*

SPEAKING OF SUPERHEROES ...

It probably won't make for an exciting comic book or Saturday morning cartoon, but the power to forgive is quite extraordinary. Lewis Smedes, an author and noted authority on forgiveness, points out that forgiveness, which is so beyond our natural ability and instincts, is as much of a miracle as walking on the water. Forgiveness definitely sounds like a superhuman quality! Perhaps when someone experiences and displays the power to forgive, they should be given a special costume. On second thought, we'd probably all look ridiculous in polyester tights.

[12] So, as those who have been chosen of God, holy and beloved, put on the heart of compassion, kindness, humility, gentleness and patience; [13] bearing with one another, and forgiving each other, whoever has a complaint against anyone; just as the Lord forgave you, so also should you forgive each other. [14] Beyond all these things put on love, which is the perfect bond of unity. [15] Let the peace of Christ rule in your hearts, to which indeed you were called in one body; and be thankful.

COLOSSIANS 3:12-14

1. What do you see as the difference between "bearing with" and "forgiving" each other (Colossians 3:13)? Which comes more naturally to you?

COMMAND 1: BEAR WITH ONE ANOTHER

2. What are some offenses where "bearing with one another" is called for? ("Bearing with" means "tolerate" or "put up with" each other.)

13As a father has compassion on his children, so the LORD has compassion on those who fear Him. 14 For He knows what we are made of, remembering that we are dust.

PSALM 103:13-14 HCSB

3. What in Psalms 103:13-14 reassures you that God understands your humanity? How can we apply this same understanding in our relationships?

While God doesn't minimize our sin, He knows we are flawed. He acknowledges our potential, as well as our limitations and weaknesses. We, likewise, would do well to make room for the humanity of others. All too often we tend to indict others for the same actions for which we'd acquit ourselves, or cut ourselves some slack.

4. Give one characteristic that you tend to forgive in yourself yet indict in others.

COMMAND 2: FORGIVE ONE ANOTHER

This command acknowledges that some people do more than annoy us.

5. What kind of offenses require "intentional" forgiveness?

In Colossians 3:12, Paul says to "put on" compassion, kindness, humility, gentleness, and patience. The image here actually suggests that we put on and wear these attributes as clothing.

6. What are some things we can infer from being told to put on the qualities in Colossians 3:12? Which of these qualities do you need to put on more often?

7. "Just as the Lord forgave you" – What do you think the point of this is? What are the full implications of this in the way you respond to people who have hurt you? How about in your relationship with God?

Paul exhorts us to *thoughtfully* and *intentionally* put on these qualities of Colossians 3:12. The act of putting them on implies that we do not in our natural state (mind and behavior) wear these qualities. When someone either deliberately hurts us or the offense go deep, it can create resentment because we feel assaulted, betrayed, or unfairly treated. Forgiveness is not natural; it's a divinely powerful weapon that we can use only because the Lord can forgive and He forgave us.

OFFENSES THAT REQUIRE FORGIVENESS

They hurt us, betray us, wound us, rob us, and sin against us. Tolerance won't do in these cases. For patience and peace to return, our response needs to be full-blown forgiveness.

We're often challenged in life to forgive people who hurt those we love. For example, we may need to forgive an in-law who abused our spouse, an insurance agent who took advantage of our parent or grandparent, a teacher who mistreated our child, or a step-parent who was cruel to our child. Forgiveness is the necessary response to many serious offenses. These offenses include (not a complete list):

- Injustice
- Deception
- Cruelty
- Humiliation
- Emotional Abuse
- Sexual Abuse
- Infidelity
- Cheating
- Betrayal
- Brutality
- Manipulation
- Slander
- Physical Abuse
- Theft
- Neglect
- And Others ...

8. Read through the list of offenses above. If you associate someone with a particular offense, write his or her first name beside that item above.

CAUTION CONTENTS FRAGILE ...

If you have names beside most of the offenses, you have too many villains. The work of forgiveness in your life will be bogged down by the number of offenders.

We cannot afford to be fragile or hyper-sensitive in our relationships. If our patience is shorter than mushrooms and our tolerance as fragile as porcelain dolls, then few, if any, of our relationships will be truly satisfying. Eventually everyone will fail to meet our unreasonable expectations because there are no margins for error.

9. Discuss this scenario: "I've resented the worship pastor ever since he didn't pick me to sing one of the solos in the Christmas musical. I need to forgive him for that." Do you think forgiveness is required in this case? Why of why not?

Unfortunately, we're hurt and offended by many things ... too many. Often, we hold on to perceived offenses. Being hurt or disappointed is natural, but forgiveness is not called for unless someone has sinned against us or hurt us intentionally. There are hurts, slights, offenses, and rejections that we may feel are unjust, but our feelings don't make those actions sinful or even wrong. We may dislike or disagree with the decisions and actions of others, but it is sin that must be forgiven. To put it bluntly, there are some things we just need to drop and move on. In short, we just need to get over it.

Forgiveness Imposters

There are several "faces" commonly put on forgiveness. We call these imposters because they misrepresent true forgiveness. True forgiveness is not associated with these imposters. Forgiveness is often misunderstood and, consequently, rejected as an option because of these forgiveness impostors:

Imposter #1: Forgiveness Forgets
When we closely link forgiveness with some form of amnesia, we discredit forgiveness as an option because we know that we can never truly forget.

Imposter #2: Forgiveness Denies
Authentic forgiveness does not deny the hurt and ignore the anger.

Imposter #3: Forgiveness Minimizes
Forgiveness does not minimize the offense. It doesn't say, "Don't worry about it; it's no big deal."

Imposter #4: Forgiveness Excuses
Forgiveness doesn't bypass the arduous journey by saying, "Oh, I know you didn't mean any harm." Toughen up, and don't just excuse the offender. Yes, the person may have meant to hurt you in some way. And that's not all right.

Imposter #5: Forgiveness Restores
Forgiveness does not always restore a relationship to what it once was. Sometimes a restoration is either not possible or not wise. We'll discover the difference between reconciliation and restoration in future sessions.

10. With which of these forgiveness imposters are you most familiar?
    Explain or give an example.

11. **Complete this sentence:** "I am most relieved that forgiveness is not _____
    _____because _____ .

EMBRACING THE TRUTH – 25 MINUTES

Standing in opposition to forgiveness imposters are the characteristics of authentic forgiveness. These characteristics represent the true nature of real forgiveness.

CHARACTERISTICS OF AUTHENTIC FORGIVENESS

(1) FORGIVENESS IS A PROCESS

Forgiveness is not an event. Although there are certainly landmark moments, it's unlikely that you will successfully dump your load of bitterness all at once. You'll probably encounter some evidence of unfinished business within the next few days, and as a result feel disillusioned about the possibility of forgiveness.

Premature forgiveness is dangerous. It denies grief or anger, and its foundation is shallow. The flimsy structure of premature forgiveness will not withstand strong winds. When we are hurt, a legitimate and necessary grieving must occur.

1. How far along would you say you are with the key stressed relationships in your life? What do you see as your greatest obstacle?

(2) FORGIVENESS CAN BE DIFFICULT

2. Is it easy to follow Jesus' commands to forgive? Explain your answer. Why do you think Jesus's commands can be difficult to execute?

Deciding to obey God and choosing to do the right thing is seldom easy to execute. Electing to climb Mt. Everest is a monumental, life-changing decision. The decision to take the initial first steps is daunting enough. The actual climb demands courage and perseverance at every step.

(3) Forgiveness Requires Supernatural Assistance

Forgiveness rubs against the grain of human nature. Even the idea of forgiving someone who has profoundly hurt us is an act initiated by the Spirit of God. Our human nature thirsts for revenge and retaliation. God is the author of forgiveness. Don't even attempt pull this off without His help.

3. In what ways have you ever experienced God's help in forgiving? What help do you need to request from Him right now?

Practical Measurements of Authentic Forgiveness

Courageous climbers of Mt. Everest know the exact location of the peak. Imagine making such a death-defying ascent with no idea about the location of the summit. Likewise, it helps us move forward in the healing journey of forgiveness when we have a clear idea of our destination. There are ways that you can know you've made significant strides toward forgiveness. Here are four measurements of authentic forgiveness:

Measurement 1: You release the right to retaliation or retribution

You choose not to get even, and you renounce the right to do so in the future.

4. How do you know when you have released the right to retaliate or seek retribution?

Measurement 2: You no longer define the offender by the offense

When the person who hurt you comes to mind, do you immediately and predominantly define him or her by the offense? Remember that forgiveness does not minimize or excuse injustice. Instead, it ceases to define the offender entirely by his or her sin. Be thankful that God does not define us by our worst or repeated sins!

MEASUREMENT 3: YOU RECOGNIZE THAT THE OFFENDER IS NOT THE TRUE VILLAIN IN THE STORY

Again, this is not an excuse for the offender's behavior; instead, it is a recognition that the offender did not act without an accomplice. People often hurt us out of their own woundedness. Ultimately, all sin is rooted in a lie. These lies include the beliefs that ...

- This behavior is right.
- This act is justified.
- This choice is reasonable.
- This action will work.

[Jesus speaking of the Devil says,] He was a murderer from the beginning and has not stood in the truth, because there is no truth in him. When he tells a lie, he speaks from his own nature, because he is a liar and the father of liars.

JOHN 8:44 HCSB

5. Who does John 8:44 identify as the true villain? What evidence identifies the true villain in your story?

Authentic forgiveness recognizes there is a spiritual battle occurring for our hearts and relationships. When we are hurt by another person, the casualty and crime scene investigations expose that the guiltiest suspects are Satan and his demonic forces, the true masterminds of the offense.

MEASUREMENT 4: YOU FEEL THE POWER TO WISH THE PERSON WHO HURT YOU WELL

The capacity to let go of the bitterness that has resulted from the injury is the fourth measurement of forgiveness. This doesn't imply that all of your negative feelings will simply vanish. Whatever pain and hurt that lingers will have an effect. Rather, the power to wish the person who hurt you well should come in steady, healthy increments along the journey. This power will allow you to move farther and farther from the offense.

6. On a scale of 1-10, how close are you currently to an injury that requires healing.

1	2	3	4	5	6	7	8	9	10

I am still very hurt
& struggling with
forgiveness

I've released my
offender & wish
him or her well,
praying regularly
for him or her

CONNECTING – 15 MINUTES

You need to be honest with yourself about where you are right now in the journey of forgiveness. There is peace in knowing the facts. Keep in mind that your group members are on journeys themselves. They will understand and accept you where you are.

LEADER INSTRUCTIONS FOR THE GROUP EXPERIENCE: Have group members take off their shoes, and exchange shoes with another group member. It's best if they exchange with a person of the same gender and/or similar shoe size. Once everyone has exchanged, instruct the group put on their "new" shoes, stand up, and walk around. After a minute or two, ask everyone to retrieve their own shoes, put them on, and return to their seats. Discuss the following questions:

1. How did your "new" shoes feel? Check all that apply.:
   - ❑ Comfortable
   - ❑ Strange
   - ❑ Different
   - ❑ Loose
   - ❑ Tight
   - ❑ Heavy
   - ❑ Light
   - ❑ Other: _____

2. Were you concerned about someone else wearing your shoes? Would you have had the same reaction to exchanging coats for a few minutes? Why or why not?

3. What does the phrase "Walking in someone else's shoes" mean to you as it relates to dealing with your offenders(s)?

4. What does the phrase "Walking in someone else's shoes" mean to you as it relates to participating in our group?

LEADER: End the discussion by saying, "The disciples were astonished and quite uncomfortable when Jesus washed their feet. Our feet are hardly glamorous or lovely. We wear socks and shoes not only to protect our feet and keep them warm, but also to cover them up. Our feet are like our stories. Everybody in this group has a story. Some chapters are not pretty, but it is our story. We need to offer each other a listening ear, an accepting hand, a compassionate voice, and a comforting shoulder. How can we support you in prayer?

MY PRAYER REQUESTS:

MY GROUP'S PRAYER REQUESTS:

In addition to specific prayer requests, pray individually for each person to begin to open up and share his or her story with the group.

Group Covenant Review:

Take time as a group to review and sign the Group Covenant on page 19. Make any adjustments that the majority of the group members, and the group leader, can support.

TAKING IT HOME

A Question to Take to God

When you ask God a question, expect His Spirit to respond to your heart and spirit. Be careful not to rush it or manufacture an answer. Don't write down what you think the "right answer" is. Don't turn the Bible into a reference book or spiritual encyclopedia. Just pose your question to God and wait on Him to answer. Focus on listening to God, and be sure to record what you hear or sense He is saying to you.

✻ Reveal to me all those whom I am guarding in the prison of my resentment. What do you want to say to me about these names? What is preventing me from taking the first step toward authentic forgiveness in these relationships?

LOOKING FORWARD ... PREPARE FOR SESSION 3

Capture your thoughts and feelings in the "Consequences Journal" on the next page, as you continue on your journey. Consider these questions to be discussed in Session 3:

1. What are some reasons that I may resist offering or even considering forgiveness?

2. What are some consequences (both external and internal) that I'm seeing as a result of unforgiveness?

3. Based on what you've learned so far, what would you list as some benefits of offering and experiencing forgiveness?

4. Why do you think God is so interested in forgiveness in your life?

CONSEQUENCES JOURNAL

The Benefits Package

Breaking the Ice – 15 Minutes

LEADER: *The "Breaking the Ice" questions will help put people at ease and continue to help them connect with each other. The first two questions ease into the discussion of benefits. The next two review the "Taking it Home" activities. Encourage everyone to participate.*

1. Imagine that you've just landed your dream job. Along with a great salary, the company has invited you to select two perks from the following list. Check the two perks that you would choose:

❏ A spacious top floor office with a panoramic view
❏ A $2,000 annual credit at the Starbucks® closest to the office
❏ Use of the company beach house in the Bahamas for a weekend every year
❏ Free annual membership in the city's most expensive gym and spa
❏ Year-round cart, green fees, and golf lessons at the area's most exclusive golf course
❏ Keys to a company car
❏ Daily 30-minute appointments with a massage therapist
❏ Weekly maid service
❏ Season tickets in the company suite for the sports team of your choice
❏ Weekly lawn service and $1,000 annual landscape credit
❏ Unlimited free babysitting on weekends
❏ One Friday and one Monday off every month
❏ Other: _____

2. Why did you choose those particular benefits?

3. Did you have a time with God discussing the people in you prison of resentment? Did you hear from God about these people or the obstacles in your journey of forgiveness?

4. You were asked to consider unforgiveness this week. What are some consequences (both external and internal) that you're seeing as a result of unforgiveness in your life or those close to you?

OPENING PRAYER

Father, we have assembled ourselves in your presence. We know you walk with us even in the darkest and most difficult times. We seek your wisdom and your revelation during this time. Help each one of us identify the way to reconciliation, and understand the blessings that await us on the other side.

OBJECTIVES FOR THIS SESSION:

- Identify reasons for resisting forgiveness, and the consequences of unforgiveness
- Grasp the benefits of forgiveness
- Realize why forgiveness matters to God, and is so important to each of us
- Move toward forgiveness by first naming the offender and offenses

DISCOVERING THE TRUTH – 30 MINUTES

Perks and benefits are great to receive. We actually expect a steady stream of benefits to flow our way in life. The truth is that almost all of our behavior is motivated either by the anticipation of rewards or the avoidance of consequences. Fortunately, God knows that we seldom act simply because something is the right thing to do. We inherently know that there are obvious or subtle benefits or consequences for all behavior. Grasping the payoffs of offering forgiveness can raise the value of forgiveness and lower our resistance to it. Likewise, when we face the negative consequences of unforgiveness, we become more inclined to consider the merits of forgiveness. Today, we move to the "ACT" step on our journey, as we discover the great benefits package that comes with forgiveness.

OUR ROUTE TO RECONCILIATION

AWAKEN: Grapple with the complexities of relationships, and the set of forces at work to disrupt and sabotage them.

→ ACT: Understand the benefits of forgiveness and my resistance; then make a decision to take the path of forgiveness, even if it's difficult.

ANALYZE: Begin to push the flywheel and inch forward by analyzing relationships and naming offenses.

RELEASE: Release is the critical juncture at which you extend compassion and gift the offender.

RECONCILE: Recognize the difference between reconciliation and restoration, readjust your heart, and then take steps to build bridges.

REBUILD: The journey to personal healing and relational reconciliation is ongoing. Continue to incorporate what you've learned through this study, what God has revealed through other channels, and the discernment that you've developed as you press on in life.

LEADER: Read the explanations and the questions for the group. Encourage everyone to participate in responding to the questions. Watch your time, and be sure to leave ample time for "Embracing the Truth" and "Connecting" segments later in the session.

ROADBLOCK AHEAD

The villain in our story places many obstacles between us and forgiveness. As a result of these obstacles, we become insensitive and less than receptive to the idea of forgiving another. Over time this lack of receptivity escalates into feelings that work to our detriment. We become insensitive not only the benefits, but also to what God wants us to do.

LEADER: Ask for a few volunteers to share in reading the following story aloud to the group:

---

³ Israel [Jacob] loved Joseph more than his other sons because Joseph was a son was born to him in his old age, and he made a robe of many colors for him. ⁴ When his brothers saw that their father loved him more than all his brothers, they hated him and could not bring themselves to speak peaceably to him.

⁵ Then Joseph had a dream. When he told it to his brothers, they hated him even more.
⁶ He said to them, "Listen to this dream I had: ⁷ There we were, binding sheaves of grain in the field. Suddenly my sheaf stood up, and your sheaves gathered around it and bowed down to my sheaf."
⁸ "Are you really going to reign over us?" his brothers asked him. "Are you really going to rule us?" So they hated him even more because of his dream and what he had said.

⁹ Then he had another dream and told it to his brothers. "Look," he said, "I had another dream, and this time the sun, moon, and 11 stars were bowing down to me." ¹⁰ He told his father and brothers, but his father rebuked him. "What kind of dream is this that you have had?" he said. "Are your mother and brothers and I going to bow down to the ground before you?" ¹¹ His brothers were jealous of him, but his father kept the matter in mind. ...

Some time after these events, Joseph's brothers were tending their father's flocks in Shechem. Jacob sent Joseph to see how his brothers were doing. Joseph caught up with the group in Dothan. ...

¹⁸ They saw him in the distance, and before he had reached them, they plotted to kill him. ¹⁹ They said to one another, "Here comes that dreamer! ²⁰ Come on, let's kill him and throw him into one of the pits. We can say that a vicious animal ate him. Then we'll see what becomes of his dreams!"

GENESIS 37:3-11,18-20 HCSB

1. Describe the feelings that Joseph's brothers had toward him. What clues in the passage reveal that these feelings were escalating?

2. What circumstances fed the escalation and fueled the brothers' hatred? What's your perspective on how Joseph treated his brothers?

3. Why do you think the brothers wouldn't forgive Joseph for the injuries they felt?

One of the factors that frequently undermines our receptivity to considering and offering forgiveness is that it **often feels like forgiveness costs us more than it benefits us**. Forgiveness is not only difficult. We can usually come up with several reasons why our bitterness is justified and forgiveness is unreasonable.

4. How do you think Joseph's brothers justified their actions in their own minds?

Resisting Forgiveness

Close your eyes and put yourself in Judah's shoes— or Simeon's or Dan's or Asher's. Your younger brother, Joseph, has come into the picture in a big, flashy way. Clearly, he is your father's favorite which is difficult enough. But more than that, he parades around in that special coat and talks about these dreams of his that seem to indicate that things won't be getting any better for you. This would be a hurtful experience—a situation the enemy is more than willing to exploit. Is this a situation warranting your forgiveness of Joseph? Of Jacob? If it were, why wouldn't you? The truth is, there are plenty of beliefs that contribute to the resistance to forgive.

5. Below are some common beliefs that cause us to resist pursuing forgiveness. Think about how these beliefs have played a role in your life. Check all that apply and discuss:

❑ If I forgive the offender, he will never understand the severity of the act.
   Counter:
❑ If I forgive, I will look weak.
   Counter:
❑ If I forgive, the offender wins.
   Counter:
❑ If I forgive, it means that I've been burned again.
   Counter:
❑ He/she doesn't deserve forgiveness, only punishment.
   Counter:
❑ Forgiveness isn't possible for this.
   Counter:
❑ The offender shows no remorse.
   Counter:
❑ The offender has not asked for forgiveness.
   Counter:
❑ The offender blames me; he believes I should forgive him!
   Counter:
❑ Other: _____

6. As a group, counter each of the beliefs in question 5 that contribute to resisting forgiveness based in God's truth in Scripture or life experience. Write these counters in the question 5 spaces.

Each of the beliefs listed in question 5 is deeply rooted in a lie that many of us have adopted as our own and lived with for, in some cases, a very long time. We must be careful not to quickly fly by these lies with intellectual counterpoints. Looking rationally at the words on a page is much different than interpreting the deeper beliefs and emotions that have been harbored in our hearts. **We'll come back to this in the "Connecting" segment.**

CONSEQUENCES OF UNFORGIVENESS

In Genesis 37, Joseph's brothers allowed their irritation of Joseph to warm, simmer, and eventually boil over into rage. Let's continue Joseph's story

²¹ *When Reuben heard this, he tried to save him from them. He said, "Let's not take his life."*
²² *Reuben also said to them, "Don't shed blood. Throw him into this pit in the wilderness, but don't lay a hand on him"—intending to rescue him from their hands and return him to his father.*
²³ *When Joseph came to his brothers, they stripped off his robe, the robe of many colors that he had on.*
²⁴ *Then they took him and threw him into the pit ... ²⁵ Then they sat down to have a meal ... ²⁶ Then Judah said to his brothers, "What do we gain if we kill our brother and cover up his blood? ²⁷ Come, let's sell him to the Ishmaelites.*

GENESIS 37:21-24,26-27 HCSB

7. What elements of this story in Genesis 37 show how vehement the brothers' rage became? To what level did these men consider the consequences of their actions?

8. Their rage was so vehement that only Reuben prevented Joseph's murder. What might have been the likely results and consequences of the brothers' failure to forgive?

Let's examine six analogies that illustrate the problematic side effects of unforgiveness.

(1) Unforgiveness is a like a ROADBLOCK that prevents you from moving forward. Your unforgiveness inhibits your own personal, spiritual, and relational growth.

(2) Unforgiveness is like a CANCER of bitterness that destroys you from the inside.
Unresolved anger turns to bitterness and hatred, which harden your heart and sabotage your capacity for joy.

(3) Unforgiveness is like a RAVENOUS BEAST – it likes the flavors of retaliation and revenge and yearns to taste them.
Unresolved resentment becomes all-consuming as it looks for a way to even the score.

(4) Unforgiveness is like SECONDHAND SMOKE – it adversely impacts those around it.
Simmering anger makes you moody, irritable, and not much fun to be around.

(5) Unforgiveness is like MONOPOLY MONEY – it can't obtain anything of real value.
Bitterness cannot produce anything positive. Why do we insist upon paying rent each day for a sink hole?

(6) Unforgiveness is like a POLITICIAN who doesn't deliver on his promises.
Resentment promises to be satisfying, but usually just makes a prisoner of the warden.

9. Which of these six analogies sounds most familiar to your experience? In which of these areas have you been hit by the enemy?

EMBRACING THE TRUTH – 20 MINUTES

LEADER: This session's "Embracing the Truth" will focus on the motivations and benefits to be found in pursuing the path of forgiveness. Guide group members to begin to integrate the truth they are discovering into their personal stories. Try to make this a personal rather than academic study.

MOTIVATIONS TO PURSUE FORGIVENESS

If forgiveness were a person who walked into your coffee shop, you'd take one look at him and say, "You're not from around here, are you?" Although we may see forgiveness as an alien from a sci-fi film, it's not an alien in this world. On the contrary, forgiveness is a powerful, helpful creature whose origin is God Himself.

1. If forgiveness walked into your life, what would it look like? What would happen?

Forgiveness comes from the nature, the very heart of God. As we consider taking the ongoing steps toward forgiveness, it's important to be aware of what should motivate us. Following are four key motivators to make forgiveness a more familiar part of our lives.

MOTIVATION 1: WE FORGIVE IN ORDER TO OBEY GOD.

God exhorts us to forgive throughout the Bible. If we flat-out refuse, we are dismissing one of God's commands. We are either saying, "The command to forgive does not apply to me in this situation," or "I don't care what God expects, I'm not going to forgive."

MOTIVATION 2: WE FORGIVE IN ORDER TO DELIGHT GOD.

Our willingness to forgive delights God. He understands how difficult it is for us to choose forgiveness. He's had considerable experience with defiant and rebellious children. Since forgiveness is so contrary to human nature, perhaps we're most like Christ when we forgive another person who has wounded us.

12 So, as those who have been chosen of God, holy and beloved, put on the heart of compassion, kindness, humility, gentleness and patience; 13 bearing with one another, and forgiving each other, whoever has a complaint against anyone; just as the Lord forgave you, so also should you forgive each other. 14 Beyond all these things put on love, which is the perfect bond of unity. 15 Let the peace of Christ rule in your hearts, to which indeed you were called in one body; and be thankful.

COLOSSIANS 3:12-14 NASB

2. What are some explicit and implicit reasons in Colossians 3 for why God commands us to forgive? In what ways is forgiveness a part of God's larger story of redemption?

MOTIVATION 3: WHEN WE CHOOSE TO FORGIVE, WE BRING GLORY TO GOD.

When we forgive someone who deserves only our disdain and complete rejection, we glorify the God who empowers us to forgive. The world expects retaliation—it's the norm. Therefore, when we encounter an episode of radical forgiveness, we are stunned by its beauty and are compelled to stare.

3. Give an example of radical forgiveness from real life, a story, a movie, or the Bible.

MOTIVATION 4: WHEN WE CHOOSE TO FORGIVE, WE HELP TO FULFILL GOD'S MISSION OF RECONCILIATION.

[17] Therefore, if anyone is in Christ, he is a new creation; the old has gone, the new has come! [18] All this is from God, who reconciled us to himself through Christ and gave us the ministry of reconciliation.

2 CORINTHIANS 5:17-18 NIV

The Bible uses the term "reconciliation" to describe Christ's work of restoring the relationship between a holy God with sin-tainted man.

4. What does 2 Corinthians 5:18 indicate that God has given us? What part does our forgiveness play in the reconciliation of God and man?

God is always at work in the world seeking to reconcile with those who have sinned against Him and rejected Him. His plan is to enlist us in that ministry of reconciliation. When we refuse to forgive, we say that we prefer to engage in the mission of division rather than cooperate with the Reconciler in His mission of restoration and reunion.

THE BENEFITS OF FORGIVENESS

As you stand on the threshold of forgiveness, you also stand on the verge of releasing its benefits. The three primary recipients of the benefits of forgiveness are you, the offender, and the relationship itself.

BENEFICIARY 1: YOURSELF

See to it that no one misses the grace of God and that no bitter root grows up to cause trouble and defile many.

HEBREWS 12:15 NIV

5. According to Hebrews 12:15, What will happen when we don't forgive from our hearts? How do you think you can benefit from forgiving someone else?

Friends, do not avenge yourselves; instead, leave room for His wrath. For it is written: "Vengeance belongs to Me; I will repay," says the Lord.

ROMANS 12:19 HCSB

6. What does it mean to "leave room for God's wrath"? Why do you think God is so possessive and emphatic about vengeance belonging to Him (Romans 12:19)?

The consequences of unforgiveness can perhaps be summed up in one word: <u>Bondage</u>. As we forgive, we take our offender off our hook and put him or her on God's hook. God is far more protective of us than we are, and He's far more qualified to avenge our hurts. As we release the desire for revenge, we can live in freedom, love, and hope. In forgiveness, we prevent a root of bitterness from destroying our hearts, joy, relationships, and freedom. When we refuse to forgive someone, we become enslaved by our own resentment. Imagine bitterness is like a fire. You can't fully live life if your purpose is to constantly stoke the eternal fire of anger and vengeance.

BENEFICIARY 2: THE OFFENDER

The second beneficiary of your forgiveness is the person who hurt you. Forgiveness gives the offender the gift of mercy and grace. Mercy is the absence or withdrawal of deserved punishment. Grace goes a step further—it does more than cancel the execution. Grace grants a pardon.

7. Think of a time when you extended forgiveness to someone, or a time someone forgave you. How did this affect the other person? How did you and do you feel about that experience?

BENEFICIARY 3: THE RELATIONSHIP

The third beneficial element of forgiveness is the possibility of reconciliation and restoration of a valuable relationship. Again, it must be said that there are cases in which a full-blown restoration of the relationship is either not possible or not wise. Bitterness is spiritual poison and must be banished for any relationship to continue.

CONNECTING - 25 MINUTES

THE GRAND PRIZE: FREEDOM

If the collective consequence of unforgiveness is bondage, then the primary benefit of forgiveness is ... **Freedom**.

It was for freedom that Christ set us free; therefore keep standing firm and do not be subject again to the yoke of slavery.

GALATIANS 5:1 NASB

[Jesus said:] I came that they might have life, and have it abundantly.

JOHN 10:10 NASB

1. According to Galatians 5:1 and John 10:10, why did Jesus sacrifice Himself for us? In what ways have you felt the bondage of unforgiveness? How could you experience freedom through forgiveness?

Earlier in this session, we discussed nine common beliefs that cause us to resist pursuing forgiveness. In question 5 on page 40, we identified those that have played a role in each of our lives. Take some time now to talk with God about your roadblocks and freedom as your leader guides you in a "listening prayer time."

LISTENING PRAYER TIME:
You're going to lead group members in a short time of listening prayer.

- *Allow this experience some time; don't rush it.*
- *Put on quiet background music (use the CD Pursued by God: Redemptive Worship Volume 1 from Serendipity House, or select your own music); dim the lights if possible.*

We are all here because we are acknowledging the struggle to forgive someone who has hurt us. We're silently confessing that we're held captive and some level by our anger or resentment. We're whispering our desire for freedom.

2. Was there anything God said to you during the "listening prayer"? Share this to encourage and help the rest of the group.

A significant step for each of us individually and as a group is to trust each other with our stories. Last week we put on one another's shoes to illustrate our common uneasiness about our feet. No one in the group is likely to be a designer footwear model. We learned that our stories are different, but we all have them, and no one's story is without pain. Today's activity is a courageous step in the journey to freedom and reconciliation.

3. Share the name of the person you're struggling to forgive and reconcile with (actual names not necessary). Also briefly cite the offense, without going into detail.

4. What did it mean to you to hear the challenges that others in the group face?

MY PRAYER REQUESTS:

MY GROUP'S PRAYER REQUESTS:

In addition to specific prayer requests, thank God now for the journey you're on together and pray for the courage to persevere.

Taking it Home

A Question to Take to God

When you ask God a question, expect His Spirit to respond to your heart and spirit. Be careful not to rush it or manufacture an answer. Don't write down what you think the "right answer" is. Don't turn the Bible into a reference book or spiritual encyclopedia. Just pose your question to God and wait for Him to speak personally in a fresh way. Be sure to write down what you hear or sense God saying to you.

* What are some of the consequences I'm experiencing as a result of my unforgiveness? What do You want to say to me about bondage and freedom?

Looking Forward ... Prepare for Session 4

Capture your thoughts and feelings in the "From My Heart Journal" on the next page, as you continue on your journey. Consider these questions to be discussed in Session 4:

1. How would you describe your own need to be forgiven by others? By God?

2. What do you think of God's command that we forgive others?

3. How would you describe the current level of your hurt and anger?

From My Heart Journal

BEGINNING STEPS

BREAKING THE ICE – 15 MINUTES

> LEADER: The "Breaking the Ice" questions will help start the session on a lighter note and continue to help the group connect a little more. Try to keep the tone upbeat and fun. To be sure everyone gets a turn, encourage people to be brief.

1. What kind of race best describes your week? Briefly explain.

   ❏ Boston Marathon – My week seemed to last forever.
   ❏ Demolition Derby – I'm all bent out of shape and beat up.
   ❏ Tour de France – I was peddling uphill one agonizing crank at a time.
   ❏ Sack Race – I fell down a lot.
   ❏ Kentucky Derby – The bell rang, the gate opened, there was a flurry of action, and then it was over.
   ❏ Indy 500 – I went 'round and 'round, and I'm right back where I started.
   ❏ Iron Man Triathlon – I had a week full of job, family, and other activities.
   ❏ 24 Hours of LeMans – Sleep? What's that?
   ❏ Downhill Skiing – I had one spectacular crash.
   ❏ Hundred Meter Hurdles – I had to sprint and deal with obstacles almost every step of the way.
   Other: _____

2. What do you think is the most difficult part of an endurance race of any kind?

3. In what ways could the process of forgiving can be compared to an endurance race?

4. Did you hear further from God this week about your bondage or the freedom to be found through forgiveness?

OPENING PRAYER

Jesus, would You prepare our hearts as we ramp up into this process of forgiveness? It is Your wish for us be forgiving people. Help us lay aside those things that may hinder our efforts, and embrace the Spirit as He guides this work in our lives.

OBJECTIVES FOR THIS SESSION:

- Recognize our own need for forgiveness
- Accept God's directive concerning forgiveness
- Acknowledge the primary motivation to pursue forgiveness
- Admit the depth of our hurt and anger
- Describe and analyze the offender and the offense

DISCOVERING THE TRUTH – 20 MINUTES

Our awareness of the benefits of forgiveness and the consequences of unforgiveness impacts our willingness to pursue forgiveness. We are ready when we have counted the cost of rage and resentment, and the payoff of forgiveness and freedom.

In this session we'll move into the "ANALYZE" step of our journey, and take the first physical steps on the healing journey toward forgiveness. We've already laid the groundwork to take these steps. As we awaken from the slumber of passivity, we'll need to recognize our own need of forgiveness, and also the depth of our feelings—anger, pain, betrayal. For some, these feelings have manifested as literal hatred. The focus of this step is work toward getting things right within ourselves, and analyzing our busted relationships.

OUR ROUTE TO RECONCILIATION

Awaken: Grapple with the complexities of relationships, and the set of forces at work
           to disrupt and sabotage them.

Act: Understand the benefits of forgiveness and my resistance; then make a
           decision to take the path of forgiveness, even if it's difficult.

⟶ Analyze: Begin to push the flywheel and inch forward by analyzing relationships
           and naming offenses.

Release: Release is the critical juncture at which you extend compassion and
           gift the offender.

Reconcile: Recognize the difference between reconciliation and restoration, readjust
           your heart, and then take steps to build bridges.

Rebuild: The journey to personal healing and relational reconciliation is ongoing.
           Continue to incorporate what you've learned through this study, what
           God has revealed through other channels, and the discernment that
           you've developed as you press on in life.

LEADER: *Read the explanations and questions for your group. Invite various group members to
read the Bible passages. Be sure to leave ample time for "Embracing the Truth," which is longer in
this session and for the "Connecting" time at the end of your session.*

THE HUMAN RACE

*¹ Since we are surrounded by such a great cloud of witnesses, let us throw off everything that hinders
and the sin that so easily entangles, and run with perseverance the race marked out for us. ² Let us fix
our eyes on Jesus, the author and perfecter of our faith, who for the joy set before him endured the cross,
scorning its shame, and sat down at the right hand of the throne of God. ³ Consider him who endured
such opposition from sinful men, so that you will not grow weary and lose heart.*

HEBREWS 12:1-3 NIV

1. Who do you think the author of Hebrews is referring to here? How might they be a
   powerful resource in your journey of forgiveness and reconciliation?

2. How does the race described in Hebrews 12:1 differ from typical competitive races? Also, how do we determine if we've won?

3. What is the key lesson we can learn from Jesus' example in Hebrews 12?

There are no scoreboard clocks or officials with stopwatches on the path to forgiveness. No one compares your speed or progress to anyone else's. Even though you should be aided and cheered on by the support and encouragement of others, forgiveness is your own private race. The race "marked out" for you is not the same as somebody else's race.

NOTE: The imagery used in Hebrews 12 is that of an athlete standing in the middle of the great stadium in Rome or another city, and looking high up at the cheering crowds that blended with the sky. For us, those who've gone before us are cheering us on saying, "You can do it! You are more than you realize!"

A Heart of Forgiveness

[21] *Then Peter came to Him and said, "Lord, how many times could my brother sin against me and I forgive him? As many as seven times?"* [22] *"I tell you, not as many as seven," Jesus said to him, "but 70 times seven.* [23] *For this reason, the kingdom of heaven can be compared to a king who wanted to settle accounts with his slaves.* [24] *When he began to settle accounts, one who owed 10,000 talents was brought before him.* [25] *Since he had no way to pay it back, his master commanded that he, his wife, his children, and everything he had be sold to pay the debt.*

[26] *"At this, the slave fell facedown before him and said, 'Be patient with me, and I will pay you everything!'* [27] *Then the master of that slave had compassion, released him, and forgave him the loan.*

[28] *"But that slave went out and found one of his fellow slaves who owed him 100 denarii. He grabbed him, started choking him, and said, 'Pay what you owe!'*

[29] *"At this, his fellow slave fell down and began begging him, 'Be patient with me, and I will pay you back.'* [30] *But he wasn't willing. On the contrary, he went and threw him into prison until he could pay what was owed.* [31] *When the other slaves saw what had taken place, they were deeply distressed and went and reported to their master everything that had happened.*

[32] "Then, after he had summoned him, his master said to him, 'You wicked slave! I forgave you all that debt because you begged me. [33] Shouldn't you also have had mercy on your fellow slave, as I had mercy on you?' [34] And his master got angry and handed him over to the jailers until he could pay everything that was owed. [35] So My heavenly Father will also do to you if each of you does not forgive his brother from his heart."

MATTHEW 18:21-35 HCSB

In this story, the king's servant had accrued an astronomical amount of debt, one that would be impossible to pay back in multiple lifetimes. Faced with being sold along with his family to repay the debt, the servant begs for more time and promises to repay the full amount.

4. What is the king's response to servant's plea for more time (verse 27)? What do you think of the king in this story? Why?

5. What is the servant's response to grace and forgiveness? How does he treat a fellow servant who owes him a miniscule amount compared to what he originally owed the king (verses 28-30)? What's your opinion of the unforgiving servant?

6. Does the king's reaction in verses 32-34 seem harsh or justified to you? Explain. What does this passage say about our refusal to forgive our "fellow servants" today?

When the servant pleaded, the king does not offer the servant more time. Instead, in a stunning move, he actually cancels the debt! The simple fact is this: We all stand in need of the same grace. The forgiveness that has been extended to each of us is the same provisional forgiveness that God has set aside for anyone who has injured you to a point that requires forgiveness. To withhold forgiveness is to withhold grace.

7. Who do you identify with most intimately from Jesus' story? Explain. How does this story from Matthew help you understand your need to forgive? How does it help you understand your need to be forgiven?

That we all require the same measure of forgiveness is the great field-leveler. This aspect of our lives puts us all on an even playing field.

EMBRACING THE TRUTH - 35 MINUTES

> LEADER: *This section will help your group members begin to integrate what can be gleaned from God's truth into their own journeys toward forgiveness.*

Although there may have been people that decided to run a marathon and were able to complete it without any training, it would be foolish to assume that this could be done. Running a marathon requires many things, not the least of which is overcoming the psychological barriers that stand in front of us, whispering, "It's too much."

The path to forgiveness preparation like any other task. With the aid of the Holy Spirit and by acknowledging and understanding these prep steps, you can break the tape at the finish line.

PREP STEP 1: RECOGNIZE MY OWN NEED FOR FORGIVENESS

As in the story of the unforgiving servant, the first step of preparation is to recognize our own need to be forgiven. If we believe that we're innocent of sin and are only victims of the sins of others, then the idea of offering forgiveness will seem absurd. Honesty and humility insist that we recognize our own flawed humanness that hurts God and other people. Famed theologian and minister G.K Chesterton was once asked, "What do you think is the primary problem with the world?" He thought for a moment and replied, "I am the problem."

[22] *There is no distinction.* [23] *For all have sinned and fall short of the glory of God.*

ROMANS 3:22-23 HCSB

⁵ God is light, and there is absolutely no darkness in Him ... ⁸ If we say, "We have no sin," we are deceiving ourselves, and the truth is not is us. ⁹ If we confess our sins, He is faithful and righteous to forgive us of our sins and to cleanse us from all unrighteousness.

1 JOHN 1:5,8-9 HCSB

1. What criteria do we typically us to compare one wrong to another? According to Romans 3 and 1 John 1, how does any of us and our wrongs compare to God?

2. After reading 1 John 1:8 and Romans 3:23, would you say that sin is an exception for people, falls on a continuum of severity and on weight scales of depravity, or is central to the human condition? Explain.

Like the indebted servant in Matthew 18, we are all in profound debt to the King whom we can never repay. We are all equally tainted with the blight of sin. It is, however, very important also to keep in mind that sin has only "tainted" us, and that we should not allow this aspect of our reality to define either ourselves or anybody else (1 John 1:9).

3. How ready are you to acknowledge that your need for forgiveness is as great as your offender's?
   - ❏ I'm not ready to buy that – I could never do to someone else what was done to me.
   - ❏ I know I need forgiveness, but my sins are still minor compared to the sins of others.
   - ❏ It's easier for God to forgive me than for me to forgive others.
   - ❏ I understand with my head, but I still hurt in my heart.
   - ❏ This is a new idea – I need to think about it.
   - ❏ I'm ready to agree with God about my sin debt and my own need for forgiveness.
   - ❏ Other: _____ .

PREP STEP 2: ACCEPT GOD'S DIRECTIVE TO MOVE TOWARD FORGIVENESS

The second preparation step is to accept God's directive to forgive. We can start the journey without complete knowledge of the entire route or certainty that we will finish it because God says to do it, and we can trust Him completely.

[23] *Jesus replied, "If anyone loves me, he will obey my teaching. My father will love him, and we will come to make our home with him.* [24] *He who does not love me will not obey my teaching.*

JOHN 14:23-24 NIV

Then [Jesus] said to them all, "If anyone wants to come with Me, he must deny himself, take up his cross daily, and follow Me.

LUKE 9:23 HCSB

[5] *Trust in the Lord with all your heart and do not lean on your own understanding.* [6] *In all your ways acknowledge Him, and He will make you paths straight.*

PROVERBS 3:5-6 NASB

4. Jesus makes strong statements to us in John 14 and Luke 9. Why is obeying God's commands and teaching so important? Is God playing the role of a demanding parent who says, "Because I said so, that's why." Explain.

5. What are the keys that you find in John 14:23, Luke 9:23, and Proverbs 3:5-6 to trusting God, to following Him even on uncomfortable paths?

The key to trust is love and abandonment. That is, we must love God enough to abandon ourselves to follow Him. The void that is left once we abandon our own selfish motives is the space that God will fill with godly desires. It's in this space that we become aware of our Father's dreams for us. If we continue to avoid this space, we will continue to follow our own, smaller dreams. Remember, God longs for us to be free!

PREP STEP 3: NAME THE OFFENDERS AND OFFENSES

The third preparation step involves explicitly declaring the offense and its damage. Fourteenth Century philosopher William of Ockham is known in certain circles for Ockham's Razor. Ockham's Razor maintains that entities should not be multiplied unnecessarily. At its essence this theory asks us to "cut away" everything not immediately a part of the equation. Basically ... "keep it simple." Employing this theory here directs you to simply and succinctly name the offender and the injury. Isolate the issue. This will allow you the opportunity to deal with the offense and subsequent healing at the purest level.

OFFENSE ANALYSIS: Your "Taking it Home" assignment this week ...

Thoughtfully and prayerfully complete this exercise. Writing your responses to the following statements will be more effective than just trying to process them in your mind. Writing will keep your mind from wandering and losing focus. Furthermore, writing will help you to clarify your thoughts and feelings as well as give you a record to refer back to later. This is a vital step, probably the most important exercise of our journey thus far.

Complete these statements:

1. The person who hurt me is _____ .

2. He/she sinned against me by: (Check all that apply.)

- ❏ Injustice
- ❏ Brutality
- ❏ Humiliation
- ❏ Physical Abuse
- ❏ Infidelity
- ❏ Other: _____

- ❏ Betrayal
- ❏ Cruelty
- ❏ Slander
- ❏ Sexual Abuse
- ❏ Neglect

- ❏ Deception
- ❏ Manipulation
- ❏ Emotional Abuse
- ❏ Theft
- ❏ Cheating

3. Describe the above sin(s) in more detail. If question 2 is the skeleton of each hurt, then this question 3 is the muscle and flesh. What do you recall about the offense(s)? Don't disguise your anger or grief. The more raw and honest you are about describing the wounds, the better your probability of healing.

4. Describe the long-term effects of the specific offenses. Sometimes an injury can cause a long-term physical or emotional change.
(Example: If you were sexually abused, you'll be angry about the abuse itself, but also about the consequences: possibly flashbacks, nightmares, low self-esteem, detachment from parent(s) who didn't believe you, distrust of people of same gender, difficulties in accepting or expressing affection, inability to be sexually secure with your spouse, etc.)

Prep Step 4: Acknowledge the Depth of Your Anger/Hate

Anger is like a warning light in your car, indicating that something is wrong, and needs to be dealt with.

[25] *Laying aside falsehood, speak the truth each of you with his neighbor, for we are all members of one another.* [26] *Be angry, and yet do not sin.*

Ephesians 4:25-26 NASB

6. The Greek word for "falsehood" in Ephesians 4:25 literally refers to the masks that were used in Greek theatre. What does this verse say about our need to be real with each other? What can happen when we keep the masks on?

7. Why do we try to hide our hurt or pain? Why is it sometimes hard to be honest about our feelings? What do you think would happen if we risked being real with God, ourselves, family, and friends ... instead of hiding behind our masks?

8. According to Ephesians 4:25 is anger okay? How can you be angry and not sin?

Your hurt, anger, and hatred are real. If you refuse to acknowledge your real feelings, you'll stay stuck where you are, and deep-seated bitterness will overpower you. Acknowledge the depth of your anger, and use it constructively without letting it master you.

Anger can be a powerful and constructive emotion when it's controlled to make positive changes. It can also be an extremely destructive emotion when it finally erupts. In order to gain control of our anger, we need to start by understanding that the primary underlying causes of anger are:

(1) **Loss of Control** – things aren't going my way or are out of control
(2) **Hurt** – betrayal, rejection, and other offenses.
(3) **Indignation** – other people are being hurt or victimized

This step in the process is focused on identifying the precise person and offense. You must know with exactness what you are forgiving and what damage it has caused. Often, the result is deep-seated anger. Honesty is paramount at this step in your journey.

9. Mark one or more of the following scales in order to get in touch with the current level of your anger. Put an X on each scale to represent how you really feel.

   When everyone is ready, share one of your responses with the group. **Caution**: Don't deny your true level of anger, but be careful not to overstate it either. You may not be as angry as others in the group. You may be angrier than many. Just tell like it is.

   a. If my anger/hatred could be measured by depth, it would be ...

   |—————+—————+—————+—————+—————+—————+—————+—————|

   So deep no man   Floating on
   will ever see it   the surface

   b. If the heat of my anger/hatred could be measured by degrees, it would be....

   |—————+—————+—————+—————+—————+—————+—————+—————|

   At the point of   Cool as a crisp
   spontaneous combustion   fall morning

   c. If my anger/hatred was a weather pattern, it would be ...

   |—————+—————+—————+—————+—————+—————+—————+—————|

   Hurricane-force winds   Gentle summer breeze

CONNECTING – 20 MINUTES

LEADER: Use this "Connecting" time to develop more closeness within your group, and to help group members connect further with their own emotions. Invite everyone to join in, and to be open and supportive of each other's struggles.

In many cases it takes an enormous effort just to overcome the shock of betrayal and emotional injury. These beginning steps are riddled with landmines and pitfalls that you must acknowledge, identify, and isolate. Dealing with the shock of being betrayed by someone you care deeply for can add to the intensity of the path to forgiveness.

1. What are you feeling after watching the events of Isaac the Bruce's betrayal?

2. How would you describe Wallace's reaction when he discovers the betrayal?

3. In what ways can you relate to Wallace? What's different for you?

My Prayer Requests:

My Group's Prayer Requests:

In addition to specific prayer requests, pray together for each person individually as he or she processes hurts and emotions this week.

TAKING IT HOME

LEADER: *Stress the vital importance of completing the Offense Analysis before your next meeting.*

OFFENSE ANALYSIS

Be sure to complete the four-step Offense Analysis on page 59 for at least one offender before your next meeting. You may use the "My Wounds Journal" on the next page, as additional space for your analysis, or use your own paper or journal.

A QUESTION TO TAKE TO GOD

When you ask God a question, expect His Spirit to respond to your heart and spirit. Be careful not to rush it or manufacture an answer. Don't write down what you think the "right answer" is. Don't turn the Bible into a reference book or spiritual encyclopedia. Just pose your question to God and wait for Him to speak personally in a fresh way. Be sure to keep a journal of what you hear or sense God is saying to you.

 ✱ After completing the Offense Analysis, I am acutely aware of my hurt, anger, and even hatred. The things going on inside me are complex and multi-faceted. What do You want to say to me about my feelings? About me?

My Wounds Journal

SEEKING TO UNDERSTAND

BREAKING THE ICE – 15 MINUTES

LEADER: Again, make these "Breaking the Ice" questions lighthearted as you start the session. You'll dive in and learn more about each other's stories from question 3 sharing about each person's Offense Analysis assignment. Watch your time. Keep sharing brief, but remember that the goal as always is to give everyone a chance to participate in responding to the questions.

1. If my family could be compared to a television show when I was growing up, it could have easily been ...

   ❏ "Saved by the Bell" – We just barely hung on.
   ❏ "Seinfeld" – It was a show about nothing.
   ❏ "The Cosby Show" – There were ups and downs, but a season for everything.
   ❏ "CSI (Crime Scene Investigation)" – It was mentally exhausting, and required a lot of attention
   ❏ "Beverly Hills 90210" – There was never a dull moment.
   ❏ "Survivor" – It was each person for himself, with betrayals and injuries.
   ❏ "The Wonderful World of Disney" – It was magical; the happiest place on earth.
   ❏ Other: _____ .

2. Which of these animals would your friends say best symbolizes how you act when you get angry? Explain.

   ❏ A stubborn mule
   ❏ A yappy, snappy, little terrier
   ❏ A coiled rattlesnake
   ❏ An attacking Rottweiler
   ❏ A sleeping lion
   ❏ An ostrich with its head in the sand
   ❏ Other: _____

3. Go around the group and briefly share some highlights from your Offense Analysis (page 59) assignment and your time with God (page 63). If you were unable to complete your analysis this week, give a couple of top-of-mind responses.

OPENING PRAYER

Spirit of God, You know our hearts and You know our stories. We invite You to walk closely with us in this process. Reveal Your ways and quiet our souls as we strive to see with eyes of understanding, seek healing, and grant forgiveness.

OBJECTIVES FOR THIS SESSION:

- Embrace the Holy Spirit's enabling power for forgiveness
- Recognize the role of understanding in forgiveness
- View the offender's past, personal issues, and intentions from a different perspective
- Become aware of deception's role in an offense
- Move toward understanding and forgiving the offender

DISCOVERING THE TRUTH – 35 MINUTES

In today's session we continue the "ANALYZE" step of our journey. The initial focus of analyzing our hurt was focused on ourselves. Now, we'll attempt to understand our offenders at on a different level and with a new perspective.

A secret to forgiveness is that it requires the ability to see any given situation through another's eyes. This requirement becomes more significant once we realize that the eyes through which we must see are those of Jesus. It's impossible to accomplish on our own.

OUR ROUTE TO RECONCILIATION

AWAKEN: Grapple with the complexities of relationships, and the set of forces at work to disrupt and sabotage them.

ACT: Understand the benefits of forgiveness and my resistance; then make a decision to take the path of forgiveness, even if it's difficult.

ANALYZE: Begin to push the flywheel and inch forward by analyzing relationships and naming offenses.

RELEASE: Release is the critical juncture at which you extend compassion and gift the offender.

RECONCILE: Recognize the difference between reconciliation and restoration, readjust your heart, and then take steps to build bridges.

REBUILD: The journey to personal healing and relational reconciliation is ongoing. Continue to incorporate what you've learned through this study, what God has revealed through other channels, and the discernment that you've developed as you press on in life.

LEADER: *To keep everyone involved, invite various members of the group to read the verses and questions aloud. This section covers several topics, so don't get bogged down, unless it's obvious that God is doing the bogging. The writing exercise in "Embracing the Truth" is very valuable, so leave some time for that, as well as for the "Connecting" discussion.*

OPTION: *You might want to consider showing the scene described in Luke 23 from the movie* The Passion of the Christ *to give people a clearer view of what occurred. Just be sure to consider the additional time required.*

A REMARKABLE UNDERSTANDING

In the days before Jesus was killed, He endured extreme suffering. From betrayal, to abandonment, humiliation, rejection, immense spiritual oppression, and merciless beatings, He saw and felt the worst of man's brutality. After His trial and sentencing, Jesus was led to a place called Golgotha, or The Skull for a brutal execution.

³³ When they arrived at the place called The Skull, they crucified Him there, along with the criminals, one on the right and one on the left. ³⁴ Then Jesus said, "Father, forgive them, because they do not know what they are doing." And they divided His clothes and cast lots. ³⁵ The people stood watching, and even the leaders kept scoffing: "He saved others; let Him save Himself if this is God's Messiah, the Chosen One! ³⁶ The soldiers also mocked Him.

LUKE 23:33-36 HCSB

1. What evidence do you see in Luke 23 that the people really did not grasp the true and complete identity of Jesus, nor the implications of their actions?

2. Had you been in His place, how do you think your response might have differed from Jesus' response to those people who deeply brutalized and humiliated Him (verse 34)?

3. What do you think was different in Jesus' perspective that enabled Him to freely forgive people hadn't asked for it, and, more importantly, did not in any way realize that forgiveness was necessary? How can we achieve this?

While the political and religious leaders acted out of self-interest to protect their power base, the crowd believed a lie. Most of the people thought they were doing the right thing by killing someone they considered to be a rebel, a blasphemer, and an impostor.

Jesus saw much deeper than the severe pain He was experiencing—into the core of what was really happening. He understood that the leadership and the public were acting from a limited understanding, and also carefully planned deceptions of the real villain in the story. This deeper understanding can make all the difference in our willingness to forgive, especially the most serious injuries.

OUT OF OUR MINDS

We'd be out of minds to think we could approach anything with Jesus' deeper understanding. We can't pull this off; we're not God. There's some truth to this, and yet, so often we don't realize or we forget all that God made accessible for Christ-followers.

[10] Now God has revealed them [hidden wisdom and mysteries] to us by the Spirit, for the Spirit searches everything, even the deep things of God. ... [15] The spiritual person, however, can evaluate everything, yet he himself cannot be evaluated by anyone. [16] For "who has known the Lord's mind, that he may instruct Him? But we have the mind of Christ.

1 CORINTHIANS 2:10,15-16 HCSB

[17] *Don't be foolish, but understand what the Lord's will is.* *[18]* *And don't get drunk with wine, which leads to reckless actions, but be filled with the Spirit.*

EPHESIANS 5:17-18 HCSB

4. According to 1 Corinthians 2:15, what special capability does the mature Christ-follower (spiritual person) possess? Why are the people around a person like this baffled by him or her?

5. In reading 1 Corinthians 2:12-16 and Ephesians 5:17-18, what would you say is the source of this special understanding or evaluation capability? Can we forgive successfully just by trying really hard? Why or why not?

6. Why is being filled with the Spirit compared to being drunk in Ephesians 5:17? According to verse 17, what's required of us to experience this filling?

As we mature in our walk with God, we are led and taught by the Spirit—the Spirit who searches and knows everything. A person filled with the Holy Spirit will likely act in abnormal ways—and that's a good thing! Neither deep understanding nor forgiveness come naturally to us. They are qualities we exhibit when we are under the intoxicating influence of God's Spirit. We truly must be out of our minds, and in the "mind of Christ."

THE POWER OF THE PAST

In the book *Ruthless Trust* (San Francisco: Harper, 2002), Brennan Manning writes, "One morning in prayer—I was an adult by this time—I had a vivid image of my now deceased mother at age six in the orphanage, kneeling on the windowsill, her nose pressed up against the glass, tears streaming down her face as she begged God to send two nice people who would adopt her. Suddenly all the anger simmering within me at my mother, all the resentment I had felt because she had not been there for me as a child, disappeared. Sobbing, I asked her forgiveness. With a radiant smile she said, " I may have messed up, but you turned out okay."

7. How did you feel as you heard Brennan Manning's story? In what ways could someone's past affect how they treat others? Discuss some examples.

8. What difference does a an offender's past have on his or her responsibility in hurting other people? How can understanding an offender's past help you forgive him or her?

People frequently hurt us because of their own woundedness. Many people have deep wounds that can be traced all the way back to their families of origin and their childhoods. They may be trying, consciously or unconsciously, to meet their needs in wrong or inappropriate ways. Or, they may be ineffectively managing their emotions.

The issues of personal history and/or family of origin do not negate the offender's responsibility or minimize our legitimate pain. Instead, they help us piece together more of our offender's story and begin to empathize with him or her.

Personal Issues

Personal issues and well-worn patterns of coping behavior also powerfully affect how people treat others. In Session 1, we recognized the ongoing spiritual battle that we're fighting with our adversary. In Session 3 we grasped the truth that Jesus came to set us free, but the adversary is still strategically working to enslave people, even people of faith.

[18] *Speaking out arrogant words of vanity they entice by fleshly desires, by sensuality, those who barely escape from the ones who live in error,* [19] *promising them freedom while they themselves are slaves of corruption; for by what man is overcome, by this he is enslaved.*

2 PETER 2:18-19 NASB

If we say, "We have no sin," we are deceiving ourselves, and the truth is not is us. 1 JOHN 1:8 HCSB

9. What enticements are used to enslave people (see 2 Peter 2:18-19)? What sign(s) tell us that people are enslaved by something or someone (verse 19)?

10. Is it accurate to say that everybody has some kind of personal issues, flaws, or character defects? Brainstorm some of the personal issues or enslavements that some people have to deal with, and how these affect the way they treat others.

Frequently, people who act out of their personal issues, bondage, or well-worn paths of coping can and do wound us. Some people may be habitually pessimistic, angry, suspicious, insecure, depressed, aggressive, passive, suspicious, insensitive, driven, controlling, skeptical, and the list goes on. Theses issues don't minimize or excuse an offender's behavior, but they help make some sense of the offense and offender. For example, an approval-seeker might neglect a spouse while desperately trying to earn favor with his employer.

INTENTIONS AND FALSE BELIEFS

Few people who wound us actually intend to hurt us so deeply. The exception is when someone seeks to retaliate against us instead of resolving an issue or forgiving us. You hurt me, so I'll hurt you back and worse. You've heard the threat—"I don't get mad; I get even."

[20] He [Jesus] said, "What comes out of a person—that defiles him. [21] For from within, out of people's hearts, come evil thoughts, sexual immoralities, thefts, murders, [22] adulteries, greed, evil actions, deceit, lewdness, stinginess, blasphemy, pride, and foolishness. [23] All these evil things come from within and defile a person."

MARK 7:20-23 HCSB

11. What does Jesus identify as the source of the evil things people do to others (verse 21)? How do these things affect the offender (verse 23)?

12. Do you think most people intend to create the level of damage they do in other's lives? What are some of the factors at work in people's lives that so pollute their hearts and innermost belief systems?

Here are a few things to keep in mind about offenders:

- Some wound out of selfishness.
- Some wound out of cowardice.
- Some wound out of ignorance.
- Some wound out of poor self-control.
- Some wound out of poor judgment.
- Some wound out of hard-heartedness.
- Some wound because they think we deserve it.
- Some wound because they are deceived.

The final point is a powerful one. Deceived people wound others. People make decisions and take action based on beliefs in their innermost being (Psalm 51:6). **Behavior, not your intellectual stance, is the best indicator of your truest, deepest beliefs.** They act out of a set of beliefs and behave according to what they falsely believe will bring relief, comfort, pleasure, success, justice, or fulfillment. Remember, Satan is the master deceiver. At the core of the events, our offender believed a lie, and subsequently hurt us.

EMBRACING THE TRUTH – 15 MINUTES

LEADER: This section will help your group members begin to integrate into their own journeys the concept of forgiveness based upon deeper understanding.

True deeper understanding of the offender and the offense comes with a set of accomplices. If the accomplices aren't present, then understanding will be more a matter of will than heart. The difference between the two is whether we go it on our own, or with the Holy Spirit working in and through us. Here are the "Understanding Accomplices":

ACCOMPLICE 1: Forgiveness with understanding requires the involvement of the Holy Spirit.

ACCOMPLICE 2: Forgiveness with understanding considers a person's past, or back story.

ACCOMPLICE 3: Forgiveness with understanding considers a person's personal issues.

ACCOMPLICE 4: Forgiveness with understanding considers a person's motives, intentions, and likely underlying false beliefs.

For many people, the insights centered in the four Understanding Accomplices unlock the ability to forgive. Your leader will ask you to spend a few minutes applying the Understanding Accomplices to your own story. Quietly and prayerfully write out your current personal responses to the following questions 1-5:

1. In what ways do I sense the Holy Spirit revealing deeper understanding to me about my offender and offense? In what ways do I need His supernatural involvement?

2. What do I know about my offender's past? What wounds or resulting patterns of behaviors or coping mechanisms may have contributed to his or her offense?

3. Are there any obvious or camouflaged personal issues or bondage that my offender has to deal with? What contribution could these issues have made to the offense?

4. Do I believe the injury was fully intentional regarding both the act itself, and the level of pain inflicted? If yes, what makes me believe that? If no, what do I think could have been some other motivations? (See examples on the previous page.)

The effort to understand the offender asks a lot of you. At the deepest levels, the ability and willingness to understand the offender isn't humanly possible. Continue to seek God on this journey and be honest at every turn.

5. How does forgiveness with Jesus' deeper understanding affect your capacity for forgiveness? If a deeper understanding of the offender is indeed helping, please elaborate on your discovery.

CONNECTING – 25 MINUTES

LEADER: This will require a willingness to share, and a deep level of trust from your members. Encourage people to carefully consider their answers and to be as honest as possible. Remind them that being a little uncomfortable is a sign of being honest in their journey to gain healing.

Share with the group key highlights of your responses to the "Embracing the Truth" questions, and then discuss the following questions with your group:

1. What have you gained by considering these questions and verbalizing your answers?

2. From among the group members, whose story resonates with you most powerfully? What is it about that story that connected with you?

3. The Bible tells us that God has put an eternity into our hearts. (See Ecclesiastes. 3:11.) By this, we are able to recognize significant aspects of our story in the world around us. What do you think you can learn from the other stories in this group?

My Prayer Requests:

My Group's Prayer Requests:

A Unison Closing Prayer

Let's invite the Holy Spirit to become an active and powerful part of our healing journeys as we read this prayer in unison:

Holy Spirit,
I surrender to you and ask for your empowerment.
In my own strength, I cannot forgive.
Using my own reasoning, I won't choose to forgive.
Invade my guarded heart. Soften my hard heart.
Speak peace to my angry heart. Heal my broken heart.
Transform my unforgiving heart.
Give me a heart that thrives in freedom.
Come, Holy Spirit,
Fill and empower me so that I might live victoriously.
Amen.

TAKING IT HOME

QUESTIONS TO TAKE TO MY HEART

Psalm 51:6 (NASB) assures us that *"You [God] desire truth in the innermost being, and in the hidden part You will make me know wisdom."* Look into your heart for what beliefs about God, yourself, and the world around you drive your attitudes and behavior. Behavior, not your intellectual stance, is the best indicator of your truest, deepest beliefs.

✳ How receptive am I really to developing a deeper understanding of my offender? What hesitation do I still have? What feelings or beliefs are at the root of my hesitation to understand more?

A QUESTION TO TAKE TO GOD

Take this question to God this week. Wait for Him to respond in a fresh and personal way.

✳ What lies or false beliefs have I harbored in my heart that have contributed to my unforgiveness? What do You see when You look at the person who hurt me?

LOOKING FORWARD ... PREPARE FOR SESSION 6

Consider these questions that will be discussed in Session 6:

1. What do you think trying to "even the score" with your offender would result in? Would this result be satisfying for you? Elaborate on your feelings.

2. If forgiveness was just a cease-fire in your relational battle, how satisfied would you be with that outcome? Would this signal for you that true forgiveness had occurred? Explain.

FORGIVENESS JOURNAL

RELEASING BOTH PRISONERS

BREAKING THE ICE – 10 MINUTES

> LEADER: It's now week six of the study and your group has shared a lot together. These "Breaking the Ice" questions should be a fun way to continue sharing your stories, and to launch the topic for today. Encourage everyone to participate in responding to the questions, but keep things moving.

Complete and briefly discuss the following statements:

1. One of the most generous gifts I ever received was _____.

2. One of the most unique or unusual gifts I ever received was _____.

3. A gift that I certainly did not expect was _____.

4. A gift I returned for a refund or exchange was _____.

5. One of my favorite moments giving someone else a gift was _____
_____.

OPENING PRAYER

Jesus, You came to set us free. There are so many that remain captives, and that are held hostage by the enemy's lies. Lord, we don't want our anger or resentment to be a part of the bondage. We want to play a role in the liberation. We ask you to bless this time, and work in our lives to release both us and the people we are struggling with as we forgive those who have caused us pain.

Objectives for this Session:

- Realize that unforgiveness will continue to hold us captive
- View examples of profound forgiveness
- Discover the role of compassion in forgiveness
- Ask Jesus to allow us to see the offender as Jesus sees him or her
- Explore the radical step of gifting the offender

Discovering the Truth – 30 Minutes

LEADER: Be sure to leave plenty of time for the personal application questions in "Embracing the Truth" and for the group experience in "Connecting" later in this session. Each of these segments contains a lot of material, so don't get bogged down in "Discovering the Truth."

Your Anger's Favorite Meal

In his book *Wishful Thinking* (San Francisco: Harper, 1993), Frederick Buechner writes, "Of the seven deadly sins, anger is possibly the most fun. To lick your wounds, to smack your lips over grievances long past, to roll over your tongue the prospect of bitter confrontations still to come, to savor to the last toothsome morsel both the pain you are given and the pain you are giving back—in many ways it is a feast fit for a king. The chief drawback is that what you are wolfing down is yourself. The skeleton at the feast is you."

The sort of anger Buechner describes is the immediate opposite of compassion. While compassion releases, bitter anger seeks to devour and control. It doesn't take much to conclude that your anger's favorite meal is you. It not only controls you, but thwarts your attempts to live the life of forgiveness and freedom you need.

In today's session we progress to the "RELEASE" step of our journey. Compassion and gifting are two radical components in the process of releasing the offender from our prison of resentment, and opening the door to a freedom we haven't known for some time.

Our Route to Reconciliation

AWAKEN: Grapple with the complexities of relationships, and the set of forces at work to disrupt and sabotage them.

ACT: Understand the benefits of forgiveness and my resistance; then make a decision to take the path of forgiveness, even if it's difficult.

ANALYZE: Begin to push the flywheel and inch forward by analyzing relationships and naming offenses.

RELEASE: Release is the critical juncture at which you extend compassion and gift the offender.

RECONCILE: Recognize the difference between reconciliation and restoration, readjust your heart, and then take steps to build bridges.

REBUILD: The journey to personal healing and relational reconciliation is ongoing. Continue to incorporate what you've learned through this study, what God has revealed through other channels, and the discernment that you've developed as you press on in life.

LEADER: In the initial part of "Discovering the Truth," you will return to the continuation of Joseph's story that was introduced in Session 3. The focus is to examine Joseph's model of forgiveness. Ask for volunteers to read the various passages and explanations. You'll also discuss three common responses to hurt.

PROFOUND FORGIVENESS

If you've ever been on the receiving end of profound forgiveness, you know what a treasured gift that is. Likewise, it is one of the greatest gifts you can give another person. Amazingly, forgiving another person is also a priceless gift to give yourself.

Let's pick up the story of Joseph and his brothers that we began in Session 3. After Joseph's brothers sold him to the Ishmaelites, they reported him as dead to their father Jacob. Through a strange series of events that only God could have orchestrated, Joseph went from slavery to being placed in charge over all of Egypt. He was second only to Pharaoh as the most powerful man in the world. Because of God's intervention, Egypt had massive grain stores when a seven-year, worldwide famine hit. Everyone came to Joseph for food during this time, including his brothers, who did not recognize him after so many years ...

[1] Joseph could no longer keep his composure in front of all his attendants, so he called out, "Send everyone away from me!" No one was with him when he revealed his identity to his brothers. [2] But he wept so loudly that the Egyptians heard it, and also Pharaoh's household heard it. [3] Joseph said to his brothers, "I am Joseph! Is my father still living?" But his brothers were too terrified to answer him.

⁴ Then Joseph said to his brothers, "Please, come near me," and they came near. "I am Joseph, your brother," he said, "the one you sold into Egypt. ⁵ And now don't be worried or angry with yourselves for selling me here, because God sent me ahead of you to preserve life. ⁶ For the famine has been in the land these two years, and there will be five more years without plowing or harvesting. ⁷ God sent me ahead of you to establish you as a remnant within the land and to keep you alive by a great deliverance. ⁸ Therefore it was not you who sent me here, but God. He has made me a father to Pharaoh, lord of his entire household, and ruler over all the land of Egypt.

⁹ "Return quickly to my father and say to him, 'This is what your son Joseph says: "God has made me lord of all Egypt. Come down to me without delay. ¹⁰ You can settle in the land of Goshen and be near me—you, your children, and grandchildren, your sheep, cattle, and all you have. ¹¹ There I will sustain you, for there will be five more years of famine. Otherwise, you, your household, and everything you have will become destitute."' ¹² Look! Your eyes and my brother Benjamin's eyes can see that it is I, Joseph, who am speaking to you. ¹³ Tell my father all about my glory in Egypt and about all you have seen. And bring my father here quickly."

¹⁴ Then Joseph threw his arms around Benjamin and wept, and Benjamin wept on his shoulder. ¹⁵ Joseph kissed each of his brothers as he wept, and afterward his brothers talked with him.

GENESIS 45: 1-15 HCSB

1. Put yourself in Joseph's place and be totally honest. If you'd been given the authority and opportunity to invoke severe revenge upon the brothers who maliciously sought to ruin your life, what would you have done? What would most people have done?

2. Joseph has the authority and opportunity to take revenge upon his brothers, but he doesn't. Why do you believe he didn't?

3. Joseph doesn't waffle between choosing to retaliate or deciding to offer forgiveness. What do you think enabled him to choose forgiveness with such definity?

4. Jesus says about His offenders, "Father, forgive them, because they do not know what they are doing." How do you see this same perspective applied in Joseph's situation as he accepts his brothers?

5. In what ways do you think Joseph shows an incredible trust in God regarding his life, and his relationships with his brothers?

Joseph had experienced some very painful losses and significant adversity throughout his life. There was plenty of time—years in fact—for him to sit alone and seethe. He *did* have options. He could have allowed his hate to consume him; just waiting for the day when he could act out of such profound anger. But when the opportunity came, there didn't seem to be any hesitation. He chose to embrace the brothers who hurt him so deeply.

Our circumstances may or may not ultimately improve as dramatically as Joseph's. In fact, we may have difficulty extracting any divine purpose or any benefit from the offense—at least in the short run. Like Joseph, however, we have a choice. We each have the same opportunity in front of us for forgiveness and compassion.

6. How can the side effects and results of the wrongs in our lives positively or negatively impact our willingness to forgive? If we are to learn from Joseph's example, what should be our driving motivations regarding the offenders in our lives?

We certainly cannot reduce Joseph's ability to forgive to a point at which he is just a nice guy caught a generous mood with the power, wealth, and control to "do something good." Rather, Joseph is spiritually and emotionally mature. In addition to evidencing a forgiving heart, Joseph shows a genuine and deep love for his brothers. Joseph acts remarkably in the face of family betrayal, false accusations, and imprisonment. He is loving and demonstrates a perspective that goes beyond his own personal comfort level. He continues to trust God despite his unfavorable circumstances.

COMMON RESPONSES TO HURT

Throughout history there have generally been three reactions to an offense or transgression. It's interesting that these same three reactions remain in our world today.

(1) TRIBALISM

Tribalism encompasses reactions on behalf of entire people groups. Typically, these reactions only escalate tension and incite violence through excessive punishment. In these cases "retaliation" would involve entire families, communities, or even nations.

7. How is this approach seen in today's global culture? In what ways do you tribalism operating in our own national or local culture. Do you see it as an effective way to deal with offenses? Explain.

(2) "EYE FOR AN EYE" JUSTICE

This approach to wrongdoing seeks to even the score. An "eye for an eye" can be understood as "you offended or injured me, so I'll respond in kind." The Old Testament standard of "eye for an eye, tooth for a tooth" was not a mandate for "get even" behavior, however. It was actually a directive to prevent tribalism in favor of a reasonable justice.

8. What do you think trying to "even the score" with your offender would result in? Would this result be satisfying for you? Elaborate on your feelings.

(3) FORGIVENESS

The grace of forgiveness looks for motivations beyond justice alone. Forgiveness, however, doesn't eliminate the natural, logical, or legal consequences for sin or violation of law. Instead, forgiveness doesn't look to punish or to settle the emotional score.

9. How is forgiveness more than just a cease-fire? In what ways do you think forgiveness is greater than justice?

EMBRACING THE TRUTH – 30 MINUTES

COMPASSION'S VITAL ROLE IN FORGIVENESS

Compassion is a genuine response to another's deep problem or need. **The first level of compassion is a heart transformation. Compassion involves looking ... really looking.**

In Session 5, we saw Jesus as the role model for compassion. Even after the betrayal, humiliation, and brutality leading up to His death on the cross, He was able to see His offenders through different eyes. He saw from a perspective altogether beyond the natural world and His own pain. Here's another example ...

35 Jesus was going through all the cities and villages, teaching in their synagogues and proclaiming the gospel of the kingdom, and healing every kind of disease and every kind of disease and every kind of sickness. 36 Seeing the people, He felt compassion for them, because they were distressed and dispirited, like sheep without a shepherd.

MATTHEW 9:35-36 NASB

1. How is compassion evident in Jesus' heart and actions in Matthew 9? What do you think drove Jesus' compassion for these people that He knew would soon betray Him?

2. It's impossible to feel compassion for someone you don't truly see him or her, looking with intention and intensity. If we truly look at our offenders with Jesus' compassion, what could happen in our hearts and actions?

Jesus peered into the windows of His offender's souls to obtain a purer understanding of their stories. True compassion allows us to see our offender with new eyes. Truly seeing into another's heart through the eyes of Jesus can be dangerous because it leads to a compassion, which makes our bitterness nearly impossible to hold on to.

In Session 2 we learned that one measurement of success along the path to forgiveness occurs when we no longer define the offender by the offense. Compassion enables this.

The Radical Step of Gifting the Offender

The second level of compassion takes us beyond the heart, and into the physical world in which we live and breathe. Although certainly radical, at least by the world's standards, gifting the offender is not the most difficult of the two levels of compassion. **Gifting the offender is an external manifestation of an internal transformation.** Let's look at an Old Testament example of gifting.

The first king of Israel, King Saul, became angry with David because God had cut off the reign of Israel from his family. Due to Saul's disobedience to God, God had selected David instead. Saul remained king until his death, but his anger swelled to hatred and an obsession to kill David. David ran from Saul for years, and several times was protected by his dearest friend Jonathan (who was Saul's son). After the death of Saul and Jonathan, David wanted to gift Saul's family …

[1] *David asked, "Is there anyone remaining from Saul's family I can show kindness to because of Jonathan?" …* [3] *Ziba [a servant of Saul's family] said to the king, "There is still Jonathan's son who is lame in both feet." …*

[6] *Mephibosheth son of Jonathan son of Saul came to David, bowed down to the ground and paid homage. David said, "Mephibosheth!" "I am your servant," he replied.*

[7] *"Don't be afraid," David said to him, "since I intend to show you kindness because of your father Jonathan. I will restore to you all your grandfather Saul's fields, and you will always eat meals at my table."*

[8] *Mephibosheth bowed down and said, "What is your servant that you take an interest in a dead dog like me?"*

[9] *Then the king summoned Saul's attendant Ziba and said to him, "I have given to your master's grandson all that belonged to Saul and his family.* [10] *You, your sons, and your servants are to work the ground for him, and you are to bring in the crops so your master's grandson will have food to eat. But Mephibosheth, your master's grandson, is always to eat at my table." Now Ziba had 15 sons and 20 servants.*

[11] *… So Mephibosheth ate at David's table just like one of the king's sons.* [12] *Mephibosheth had a young son whose name was Mica. All those living in Ziba's house were Mephibosheth's servants.* [13] *However, Mephibosheth lived in Jerusalem because he always ate at the king's table. He was lame in both feet.*

2 Samuel 9:1-13 HCSB

3. What is the specific nature of David's gift to Mephibosheth (verse 7)? What explicit reason does David give for his generous gift (verses `1 and 7)?

4. In verse 1, David requests "anyone remaining from Saul's family." What is the underlying message in David's gift with regard to Saul's offenses toward him? How are David and Mephibosheth co-beneficiaries of the gift (verses 11-15)?

5. How would you have responded to King David had you been Mephibosheth in that moment of gifting? Describe how this might have changed your life.

David had every right to hold a grudge against Saul, but instead extends a generous and personal gift to Mephibosheth. It was more than just an expression of memorial kindness to Jonathan. His gift is also his expression of forgiveness to Saul.

8 Live in harmony with one another; be sympathetic, love as brothers, be compassionate and humble. 9 Do not repay evil for evil or insult for insult, but with blessing, because to this you were called so that you may inherit a blessing.

1 PETER 3:8-9 NIV

6. What are some key perspectives, listed in 1 Peter 3:8-9, that we need to ask God to instill in us so we are able to forgive, and walk through a healthy forgiveness process?

7. How does 1 Peter 3:8-9 present the concept of gifting as an outward expressions of an inner change? How do you think the double blessing might work?

GIFT IDEAS FOR A GESTURE OF FORGIVENESS

Dr. Robert Enbright, noted expert on forgiveness, offers these suggestions as possible gifts:

- **Greeting Card:** Send a greeting card on a holiday, birthday, Father's Day, Mother's Day, etc. Even without writing content, the kind gesture alone is an expression of forgiveness.

- **Thank-You Note:** Send a note that expresses gratitude for something good the person has done.

- **Gift Certificate:** Invite the recipient to enjoy something of his or her choice at a favorite store or restaurant.

- **Handmade Gift:** A gift is especially meaningful and personal if you make it.

- **Invitation:** Invite the recipient to a meal, birthday party, memorial service, or graduation.

- **Time or Presence:** A person's time, in this case yours, is often recognized as a gift. For example, an incest survivor visited her dying father in the hospital. She gave him the gift of her time and presence as she spent long hours sitting by his bed, and later feeding him.

There are, of course, many other gift ideas. Your choice to gift the offender in even the most minor way can be understood as an outward demonstration of an inner release.

8. At what level are you ready to gift your offender?

❏ Not yet ready
❏ Greeting Card
❏ Thank-You Note
❏ Gift Certificate
❏ Hand-made Gift
❏ Invitation
❏ Time or Presence

9. How would your offender likely respond to your gift? In what ways are you prepared and/or unprepared to handle this?

10. How would "gifting" benefit you and contribute to your freedom?

CONNECTING – 20 MINUTES

1. How could Jean Valjean possibly justify stealing the silver after he was shown such hospitality and generosity by the priest?

2. How could the priest forgive someone who rewarded his initial compassion with theft and violence?

3. The priest did not send Jean Valjean back to prison, but instead gifted him with the silver and the silver candlesticks. How did you feel as you watched this scene?

4. Both the priest and his wife were relieved to see Jean Valjean returned by the authorities, but for different reasons. How does the contrast between the man and woman illustrate the differences between justice and grace?

6. What do you think the priest wants to give Jean Valjean that is far more valuable than silver?

7. What do you see in Jean Valjean's face at the end of the scene? Share any remaining concerns about which the group can pray.

My Prayer Requests:

My Group's Prayer Requests:

In addition to specific prayer requests, thank God for His gift of grace and mercy. Ask Him to give each of you the courage to extend that gift to your offenders.

TAKING IT HOME

A QUESTION TO TAKE TO MY HEART

Look into your heart for the answer to the following question. This is introspection time—time to grapple with what drives your thinking and behavior, with what you believe in the deep recesses of your heart about God, yourself, and the world around you. Your behavior, not your intellectual stance, is the best indicator of your truest, deepest beliefs.

✳ How ready am I really to truly "see" my offender with the eyes of Jesus? What's preventing me from being compassionate toward him or her—to bless instead of curse? What core beliefs do I need to ask the Holy Spirit to transform?

LOOKING FORWARD ... PREPARE FOR SESSION 7

Capture your thoughts and feelings in the "Reconciliation Journal" on the next page, as you work through the reconciliation process. Consider these questions to be discussed in Session 7:

1. How would you describe the difference between reconciliation and restoration??

2. How do you think we can determine or discern with whom we should pursue or not pursue reconciliation? How about restoration? Give some examples.

Reconciliation Journal

RECONCILIATION & RESTORATION:
THINKING ABOUT THE UNTHINKABLE

BREAKING THE ICE – 10 MINUTES

LEADER: *After a brief "Breaking the Ice," you'll jump right into a unique group experience.*

1. If a judge gave my ex-spouse jail time for how much he or she has hurt me (and my family), I think he or she would be sentenced to:

   ❏ Probation and community service
   ❏ 1 week in jail and $5,000 fine
   ❏ 1 year in county jail with laundry duty and no TV privileges
   ❏ 2 years in jail with one month of solitary confinement
   ❏ 5-10 years in the state penitentiary
   ❏ Life sentence with no chance of parole
   ❏ Other: _____

2. How did your week go? What progress have you made in being able to see your offender with deeper understanding?

LEADER: Locate a copy of Lewis Smedes' book Forgive and Forget: Healing the Hurts We Don't Deserve (San Francisco: Harper, 1997) *notation & recommendation). Read aloud "The Magic Eyes: A Little Fable," which is found in the introductory section of Smedes' book. This reading will prime the following group experience and discussion.*

"EYES OF JESUS" GROUP EXPERIENCE – 20 MINUTES

LEADER INSTRUCTIONS FOR THE GROUP EXPERIENCE: It would be most effective to have ropes draped on an empty chair for each group member, as well as a soft foam baseball bat or foam tube. Ask all group members to stand next to the empty chairs, and then walk all of them through this exercise at the same time. Encourage people to listen and thoughtfully follow along with you, as they focus only on their own situation.

Say, "This week you'll complete a powerful and deeply spiritual forgiveness exercise described by Christian therapist, Dr. Gary Moon, in his book Falling For God *(Shaw, 2004). I'm going to ask you all to stand together, with each of you selecting an empty chair near you. Please focus on you own situation as I lead you through this experience.*

EYES OF JESUS

Close your eyes and imagine that you walk into a small prison cell. It has cement floors and cinder-block walls. Picture the villain, your offender, sitting on a chair in the middle of the room. The ropes binding his or her legs and arms to the chair prevent escape or movement. The only other item in the room is a wooden club propped up in the corner. Recall the offense and feel your anger and disgust.

(1) See yourself walk over and pick up the club. Feel the handle and the barrel of the club in your hands. Then, walk over to where the offender is sitting in the chair and raise the club over your head to strike him or her. Just as you are about to bring the club down the head, you remember that a Christian is supposed to forgive, so you drop the club and say, "I forgive you. I must." Then you walk away. Your anger, however, still simmers. Your words of forgiveness are premature, hollow, and even artificial.

(2) Next, imagine a second scenario. You're standing over the offender with the club again raised and poised to strike. Your anger says, "Pay this jerk back ... after all, the Bible says an eye for an eye." You answer your anger by saying, "Yes. This is justice!" and you beat the offender with the club. You feel great as you release your anger, and retaliate for the way this person has hurt you. But, the relief passes quickly. The retaliation is not as gratifying as you'd hoped.

(3) Now, imagine a third alternative. You're standing over your offender with the club raised above your head. As you stand there poised and ready to retaliate, you recount the pain you have experienced because of the offense. Allow yourself to experience the pain again, right here and now. You know that in terms of justice alone, you have the right to hurt this person for the pain he or she has caused you. You feel the pain and say nothing. You do not give into a premature declaration of forgiveness. You understand that true forgiveness is not denial, repression, or retaliation. Therefore, you resist the temptation for payback. You stand ready to strike, feeling the pain, but you do nothing more.

(4) Finally, imagine that Jesus enters the room and walks over by your side. You say, "Jesus help me. I don't want to pretend that I'm not dying inside, and I don't want to make things worse. I want to be free. Help me, please. I want to hit this person so much, but I know it's the wrong thing to do." Now, ask Jesus to speak to you. Be still and listen.

LEADER: *After giving group members a few minutes to listen to Jesus, ask them spend a few more minutes journaling about this experience. If anyone is willing to share, allow time for that too.*

Note: Don't be surprised or discouraged if your first attempt at this exercise doesn't feel successful. Try this again at home. It's imperative that you're in a quiet and private place with sufficient time. Do not rush this. Really make an effort to engage in this exercise this week. Of course, if for some reason your genuine attempts seem to fall flat, do not give up on the validity of the exercise. Try again in the near future.

Record the actions and words of Jesus here, along with your thoughts, and feelings.

This is the true story of Kathy's experience as she went through this spiritual exercise.

When Kathy asked Jesus to speak to her, her husband, Brad, was in the chair. Her club was poised to strike an unfaithful spouse. Jesus looked into her eyes, and she felt deeply loved. Slowly her arms came to rest at her sides. Still lost in Jesus' gaze, she dropped the club. I know you are hurting so badly, she felt Jesus say. But look at Brad now.

Kathy looked at where Brad had been sitting, tied to the chair, but what she saw surprised her. She saw an eight-year old boy holding a football trophy with tears sliding down his cheeks. Somehow she recognized Brad's deep fear, and sensed the deep truth that he was not a monster that wanted to devour, but a little boy who just wanted to be loved and had no idea how to make that happen.

"He's just like me," she sobbed aloud.

Then she felt Jesus say to her, "I want to be with you both. I want to love you and teach you both how to love."

Jesus took her by the hand, but her hand was small. She was a little girl. Together, Kathy and Jesus knelt by the little boy and untied the ropes.

"Do you want to play with me?" the little boy asked after being untied.

"Yes, we do" she said.

OPENING PRAYER

Spirit of God, give us discernment today. As we pursue our journey of forgiveness, we ask You to light the path before us and make our destination clear. Although we seek reconciliation and restoration, our ultimate aim is to sense Your presence in our hearts and join You in the journey of forgiveness.

OBJECTIVES FOR THIS SESSION:

- Understand the difference between reconciliation and restoration
- Investigate heart attitudes that promote or block forgiveness and reconciliation
- Realize that reconciliation or restoration is not always possible or wise
- Discover when reconciliation and restoration is possible, wise, and mutually desired
- Write a letter of forgiveness (that won't be sent) to your offender

DISCOVERING THE TRUTH – 25 MINUTES

Throughout our study of *Radical Reconciliation*, you've charted some progress each week on Our Route to Reconciliation. Tracking progress indicates that the journey of forgiveness has a destination. The ideal destination is personal freedom and reconciliation or restoration of the relationship. We don't live in a world of ideals, however. There will be times when the Route to Reconciliation is a personal journey only. Although your heart and mind may be reconciled, in some cases it is neither advisable nor wise for the journey to culminate with restoration. In this session we move forward into the "RECONCILE" step of Our Route to Reconciliation. We'll explore the meanings of both reconciliation and restoration as we move thoughtfully down the road.

LEADER: In "Discovering the Truth," you will see a powerful illustration of reconciliation and restoration in the story of the Prodigal Son. Ask for volunteers to read various Bible passages and explanations. It would make it more engaging if you ask four members to read the passage in parts. Keep things moving at a steady pace through "Discovering the Truth" and "Embracing the Truth." Leave ample time for another group experience in the "Connecting" time.

Our Route to Reconciliation

AWAKEN: Grapple with the complexities of relationships, and the set of forces at work to disrupt and sabotage them.

ACT: Understand the benefits of forgiveness and my resistance; then make a decision to take the path of forgiveness, even if it's difficult.

ANALYZE: Begin to push the flywheel and inch forward by analyzing relationships and naming offenses.

RELEASE: Release is the critical juncture at which you extend compassion and gift the offender.

RECONCILE: Recognize the difference between reconciliation and restoration, readjust your heart, and then take steps to build bridges.

REBUILD: The journey to personal healing and relational reconciliation is ongoing. Continue to incorporate what you've learned through this study, what God has revealed through other channels, and the discernment that you've developed as you press on in life.

RADICAL RECONCILIATION ILLUSTRATED (LUKE 15:11-32 HCSB)

Jesus told a story to illustrate God's love and forgiveness for us no matter what we've done. This story of the Prodigal Son also gives us insights into our own relationships.

NARRATOR:
[11] *A man had two sons.* [12] *The younger of them said to his father,*

YOUNGER SON:
"Father, give me the share of the estate I have coming to me."

NARRATOR:
So he distributed the assets to them. [13] *Not many days later, the younger son gathered together all he had and traveled to a distant country, where he squandered his estate in foolish [or loose] living.* [14] *After he had spent everything, a severe famine struck that country, and he had nothing.* [15] *Then he went to work for one of the citizens of that country, who sent him into his fields to feed pigs.* [16] *He longed to eat his fill from the carob pods the pigs were eating, but no one would give him any.* [17] *When he came to his senses, he said,*

YOUNGER SON:
"How many of my father's hired hands have more than enough food, and here I am dying of hunger! [18] *I'll get up, go to my father, and say to him, 'Father, I have sinned against heaven and in your sight.* [19] *I'm no longer worthy to be called your son. Make me like one of your hired hands.' "*

1. What did the younger son (prodigal) do that required the father's forgiveness (verse 13)? Do you think the son experienced a real change of heart? Explain.

2. In verse 19, the son says "I'm no longer worthy to be called your son." Do you believe he deserves forgiveness and reconciliation? How about full restoration? Discuss responses.

NARRATOR:
[20] So he got up and went to his father. But while the son was still a long way off, his father saw him and was filled with compassion. He ran, threw his arms around his neck, and kissed him. [21] The son said to him,

YOUNGER SON:
"Father, I have sinned against heaven and in your sight. I'm no longer worthy to be called your son.'"

NARRATOR:
[22] "But the father told his slaves,

FATHER:
"Quick! Bring out the best robe and put it on him; put a ring on his finger and sandals on his feet. [23] Then bring the fattened calf and slaughter it, and let's celebrate with a feast, [24] because this son of mine was dead and is alive again; he was lost and is found!"

3. Was there anything surprising to you in the father's reaction? What caused the father to react to his prodigal son the way in which he did?

4. How might you had responded in this situation? How do you think the son must have been feeling at this point?

5. How would you explain the difference between reconciliation and restoration? Which of these did the son expect? Which did he receive from his father?

In this story, the son hopes for a reconciliation with his father ("Make me like one of your hired hands"), but dares not hope for a full restoration of his status as son ("I'm no longer worthy to be called your son"). However, because of his loving, gracious, forgiving father, the son gets more than he ever dreamed he would get. His relationship with his father is fully restored!

Reconciliation is a mutual truce, a peace treaty of sorts. There's a level of reconnection of the relationship with reconciliation, but there may not be an intimate and deep reunion. Reconciliation is a significant breakthrough in the forgiveness journey!

Restoration, on the other hand, is a mutually desired and agreed upon rebuilding of the relationship. Closeness is sought and valued. Where reconciliation may be described as repairing the relationship and moving on (perhaps separately), restoration is healing the relationship and moving on together.

6. What in the passage reveals that the father truly forgives his son? What reveals that he invites him beyond reconciliation and into restoration of their relationship?

7. What words might the Prodigal Son use to describe the restoration?

NARRATOR:
So they began to celebrate. [25] *Now his older son was in the field; as he came near the house, he heard music and dancing.* [26] *So he summoned one of the servants and asked what these things meant.*
[27] *"Your brother is here," he told him, "and your father has slaughtered the fattened calf because he has him back safe and sound."* [28] *Then he became angry and didn't want to go in. So his father came out and pleaded with him.* [29] *But he replied to his father,*

OLDER SON:

"Look, I have been slaving many years for you, and I have never disobeyed your orders, yet you never gave me a young goat so I could celebrate with my friends. ³⁰ But when this son of yours came, who has devoured your assets with prostitutes, you slaughtered the fattened calf for him."

FATHER:

³¹ "Son, ... you are always with me, and everything I have is yours. ³² But we had to celebrate and rejoice, because this brother of yours was dead and is alive again; he was lost and is found."

LUKE 15:11-32

8. Toward whom is the older brother targeting his resentment (verses 29-30)? What's the source or cause of the eldest son's bitterness?

9. What do you see as the deep down reason that blocks the older son's ability to reconcile with his younger brother? How about with his father? What behavior(s) reveal the eldest son's deepest core beliefs about his father, his brother, and himself?

The father restores the relationship with the younger son and desires that his eldest son at least reconcile with his younger brother. However, the eldest son will have no part in it. This is symbolized by his refusal to join the party. He chooses to hold on to his bitterness toward his brother and his father. In fact, because of his father's desire for a reconciliation to occur, he resents his father even more now. Likewise, you may discover that as you move to reconcile or restore a severed relationship, some people close to you may criticize or even oppose your effort. The irony in the eldest son's situation is that while the younger son was many physical miles away from his father, the elder son was as many miles away emotionally. In the end, the younger son returns, but the elder son actually increases his distance from his brother and father.

EMBRACING THE TRUTH – 20 MINUTES

16 Be in agreement with one another. Do not be proud ... Do not be wise in your own estimation. 17 Do not repay anyone evil for evil. Try to do what is honorable in everyone's eyes. 18 If possible, on your part, live at peace with everyone. 19 Friends, do not avenge yourselves; instead, leave room for His wrath. For it is written: "Vengeance belongs to Me; I will repay," says the Lord.

ROMANS 12:16-19 HCSB

1. A destructive cycle begins when people hurt us, and we in turn hurt them. According to Romans 12, what key attitudes and actions help us break out of this destructive cycle?

2. What responsibility does the statement, "If possible, on your part, live at peace with everyone" leave for us? What release or relief do you see in this same statement?

3. In Session 3, we discussed what it means to "leave room for God's wrath." Why is God so possessive and emphatic about vengeance belonging to Him (verse 19)?

This journey of forgiveness takes time, but once we've allowed ourselves to truly feel anger, sadness, and hurt, then the next step is to begin to move toward forgiveness. As we do that, we take our offender off our hook, and put him or her on God's. As we discussed earlier in this study, God is far more protective of us than we are, and He's far more qualified to avenge our hurts. As we release the desire for revenge, we can live in freedom, love, and hope. In forgiveness, we prevent a root of bitterness from imprisoning our hearts.

The Heart of Restoration

Like the complete reunion between the Prodigal Son and his father, restoration reflects the heart of Jesus who restored us to relationship with our Father. Such healthy and lasting restorations are possible when they are in the best interests of all involved, and when they are mutually desired.

4. How do you think we can determine or discern with whom we should pursue or not pursue reconciliation? How about restoration? Give some examples.

Sometimes a reconciliation or restoration is not wise or in the best interests of one or both parties. For example, there are times when resuming the relationship could be dangerous. There are relationships too volatile, unstable, or destructive. We'll discuss this further in Session 8.

5. What is likely result from relational restoration? What are some ways we can be sure that restoration has occurred?

Restoration is not always as dramatic and ceremonial as the return of the Prodigal Son. It's possible that neither side will call much attention to an official restoration of the relationship. Frequently, the restoration begins with forgiveness and moves tentatively toward re-trusting and reunion over a period of time. The restoration progresses slowly and gradually.

6. What experiences do you have that might help in the process of reconciliation, and maybe ultimate restoration?

CONNECTING – 15 MINUTES

LEADER INSTRUCTIONS FOR THE GROUP EXPERIENCE: There is a great scene from the film Legends of the Fall *(Brad Pitt, Anthony Hopkins, Aiden Quinn) that serves as a dramatic illustration of the Prodigal Son story. Read the following paragraph, and then begin in Scene 24 (from 54:56 to 57:23 minutes on the DVD) as Tristan returns, riding back through the field to his home toward the reunion with his father. After viewing the scene, engage the group through the questions that follow.*

In the film *Legends of the Fall* (Brad Pitt, Anthony Hopkins, Aiden Quinn), we see a dramatic illustration of the Prodigal Son story. Tristan (Brad Pitt) is the youngest of three sons. He is charismatic, handsome, and untamed. The older son is responsible, successful, respected, and resentful of Tristan's status as the favorite. Prior to the scene we'll watch, Tristan has been away from home for several years. He has communicated with no one during his absence—including his father (Hopkins). He returns home to find that his father has suffered a stroke.

1. How is this scene similar to the Parable of the Prodigal Son? Are the effects of each similar? Discuss your responses.

2. What did you feel when you saw the father's reaction to his son's return? Did this stir any longings inside you? Explain.

3. If you could have the real desire of your heart in your difficult relationship, what would it look like? Why do you think that's important to you?

How can this group pray for and support you as you take the next step in your route to reconciliation?

MY PRAYER REQUESTS AND SUPPORT NEEDS:

MY GROUP'S PRAYER REQUESTS AND SUPPORT NEEDS:

In addition to specific prayer requests, thank God for giving us Jesus, who made restoration with our Father possible, and showed us the way to humbly reconcile.

IMPORTANT LEADER NOTE: *Be sure to highlight the letter each person needs to write before your next meeting.*

TAKING IT HOME

A QUESTION TO TAKE TO GOD

When you ask God a question, expect His Spirit to respond to your heart and spirit. Be careful not to rush it or manufacture an answer. Don't write down what you think the "right answer" is. Don't turn the Bible into a reference book or spiritual encyclopedia. Just pose your question to God and wait for Him to speak personally in a fresh way. Be sure to write down what you hear or sense God saying to you.

✳ God, how am I like the father in the story of the Prodigal Son? In what ways am I like the older brother? What patterns in my behavior do I need to pay attention to so that I can move ahead?

A LETTER TO RELEASE MY HEART

This week you're encouraged to write a letter offering forgiveness to the person who hurt you. The value of this exercise will be in expressing yourself through the process and taking further steps to release your captive heart.

It's really okay if you haven't fully forgiven the person. Just be honest, and write about where you currently are in the healing journey.

Begin by saying something like "Dear _____, This is awkward for me, so bear with me ..." Your letter must include a general description of the offense, your honest reactions to it, and your consequent feelings about the person. Your letter should also include a sense of your movement toward forgiveness. There's a loose, suggested structure to get you started on the next page.

You'll be invited to read your letter to the group in our final session next week, so please remember to bring it with you. Put it in your Bible or book so it's sure to make the trip.

My Letter of Forgiveness

I was really hurt when you _____.

It made me really angry when you _____.

Before that happened, I thought we were _____.

Since it happened, I have been _____.

You probably have no idea how _____.

I've secretly wished _____.

It has been hard to forgive you because _____.

I've embarked on a journey toward forgiveness because _____.

God has helped me to see that _____.

One way that God has helped me to see you differently is _____.

I know that I'm making progress toward truly forgiving you because _____
_____.

When you read this I hope that you will _____.

I hope that we can _____.

_____

_____

_____

_____

_____

_____

_____

_____

_____

_____

_____

_____

_____

_____

_____

_____

_____

RADICAL RELEASE!

BREAKING THE ICE – 15 MINUTES

1. As you think about radical release which experience sounds most freeing to you? Explain your choice.

   ❏ Parasailing – Soaring over the deep blue
   ❏ Bungee jumping – Hurtling head first and bounding back
   ❏ Space shuttle – Pulling G's at launch and busting through the atmosphere
   ❏ Parachuting – Free-falling out of the clouds
   ❏ Indy 500 – Pedal to the floor in a Formula One racecar
   ❏ Skiing – Gliding through the packed powder on a Black Diamond slope
   ❏ Cycling – Flying down the open road
   ❏ Other: _____

2. Briefly describe the most radical thing you've ever done.

3. OPTIONAL: James 1:5 says, "If any of you lacks wisdom, let him ask of God." After listening to the song, what are you daring to ask God for?

OPENING PRAYER

Dear Lord, thank you for this time. Thank you for blessing us and giving us new eyes. Though the journey isn't over—for some of us it's only begun—we know that you will continue to reveal Yourself as we seek healing; that You will release us as we seek freedom.

OBJECTIVES FOR THIS SESSION

• Share with group members the "letter of forgiveness" you composed
• Discern when restoration is either not possible or not wise
• Address some remaining questions and dilemmas regarding forgiveness
• Review and share helpful principles from the entire series
• Affirm the group members in their continued healing journey of forgiveness

---

LEADER NOTE: *This would be a good time to ask the group if they would like to continue meeting for continued support. Remind them that their journeys are only beginning, and that the group has a great start toward becoming a redemptive community. Pass around 3 x 5" index cards so people can jot down their potential interest. Some of the group members may be open to the idea.*

If there are not enough to form a small group, refer these people to your pastor to connect them with a group. If you form a group, we suggest your next step be to go through the Serendipity House study entitled Great Beginnings. *You may order this online at www.SerendipityHouse.com.*

DISCOVERING THE TRUTH - 30 MINUTES

Even though we're coming to the end of our study, your forgiveness journey is not complete. You've encountered the benefits of forgiveness and the effects of unforgiveness. You can define authentic forgiveness and tell what it's not. Perhaps you've embraced the pursuit of freedom that forgiveness brings. You've perhaps been honest about the depth of your anger, and have been challenged to see your offender with understanding and compassion. If you've engaged thoughtfully in this group, you now know how to measure your progress toward forgiveness. Some of you are ready to begin the courageous steps toward reconciliation and restoration. Keep reviewing the truth of this study.

In this final "REBUILD" session we'll seek to address several other issues regarding forgiveness. At the end of this session, we'll find some release in a meaningful experience.

OUR ROUTE TO RECONCILIATION

AWAKEN: Grapple with the complexities of relationships, and the set of forces at work to disrupt and sabotage them.

ACT: Understand the benefits of forgiveness and my resistance; then make a decision to take the path of forgiveness, even if it's difficult.

ANALYZE: Begin to push the flywheel and inch forward by analyzing relationships and naming offenses.

RELEASE: Release is the critical juncture at which you extend compassion and gift the offender.

RECONCILE: Recognize the difference between reconciliation and restoration, readjust your heart, and then take steps to build bridges.

REBUILD: The journey to personal healing and relational reconciliation is ongoing. Continue to incorporate what you've learned through this study, what God has revealed through other channels, and the discernment that you've developed as you press on in life.

LEADER: This is a vulnerable moment. It is difficult to read something so personal out loud. Let the group know that it is natural to feel anxious about what others think about the letter.

---

1. Last week you were encouraged to write a letter offering forgiveness to the person who hurt you. It's not necessary for you to send the letter. The value of the letter is to clarify and express your thoughts, feelings, and hopes. **Please read your letter to the group.**

NOTE: After each group member reads his or her letter, the rest of the group should briefly affirm the letter and the reader. Qualities that can be affirmed include courage, honesty, insight, compassion, transparency, vulnerability, humility, and gentleness.

HOW FAR AND HOW LONG?

LEADER: Read the explanations between the questions for the group. Encourage everyone to participate in responding to the questions. Invite volunteers to read the various Bible passages. Be sure to leave extra time for the "Connecting" segment at the end of your time together.

One question that might be hanging in the air is, "How far should I go with forgiveness?" If this question has been on your heart, just know you're not the first and you wont' be the last to ask. Peter asked the same of Jesus. There will continue to be questions. This will always be the case in matters of the heart.

²¹ *Then Peter came to Him and said, "Lord, how many times could my brother sin against me and I forgive him? As many as seven times?"*
²² *"I tell you, not as many as seven," Jesus said to him, "but 70 times seven.*

MATTHEW 18:21-22 HCSB

When we come to the table of forgiveness, we have many questions. Peter's question reveals his concern about expectations and limits. We're not sure what prompted Peter's inquiry. In the Jewish tradition, forgiving three times was considered quite sufficient. Peter doubles it and adds one. He possibly came up with the number seven because it was considered the perfect number in Jewish tradition.

1. Peter asked a reasonable question. What problems do you see with Peter's question?

2. What questions do you still have at this point that we can discuss as a group?

Peter makes the issue one of forgiving a brother. In Peter's time, the prevailing tradition was that a Jew was not obligated to forgive a non-Jew. In the Parable of the Good Samaritan, Jesus confronts the narrow religious definition of neighbor. Clearly Jesus implies that all are brothers and neighbors when the issue is doing what's right. Peter is very preoccupied with the legal aspects of forgiveness. It's as if he wants the number of times to which he is obligated to try. We're back to score-keeping. As always, Jesus' response will always ask us to broaden our minds, and extend the reach of our hearts.

3. How has Jesus' response challenged you during the past few weeks?

UNFORTUNATE SABOTAGE

If possible, on your part, live at peace with everyone.

ROMANS 12:18

When possible, we should seek reconciliation and restoration of broken relationships. However, there are times when neither may be achieved.

4. What is Paul saying we should do in Romans 12:18? What if somebody won't even give us the time of day?

Paul recognizes that it's not a one-way street. It takes two to make a relationship work, but it only takes one to sabotage it. The truth is that some people will not let you live at peace with them. On these occasions we must accept the blockage. However, we still offer forgiveness, whether or not it's accepted or even valued.

Reconciliation is not possible when it is completely blocked by the other person. There are also other instances in which either reconciliation or restoration are not likely to occur. First, although partial reconciliation may be possible, complete reconciliation is not possible with someone who is deceased. Ultimate restoration is not possible when an ex-spouse has remarried even though the relationship may be reconciled.

5. How is a form of reconciliation possible with someone who is absent or even deceased?

Not Wise

Although reconciliation may be a noble and obtainable goal, time for restoration remains in the future in some cases. Sometimes reconciliation or restoration is not wise or in the best interests of one or both parties. For example, there are times when resuming the relationship could be dangerous.

6. Give some other examples of relationships that should not be reconnected too quickly.

- Relationship with someone who has an addictive behavior and is not actively seeking help from someone other than you
- Relationship with someone who cannot control his or her anger
- Relationship with someone who may put your safety or your children's safety at risk
- Relationship with someone who is dishonest
- Relationship with someone who is emotionally or verbally abusive
- Relationship with someone who knowingly tempts you to do wrong

7. What kinds of issues can develop when people prematurely reconcile?

Premature reconciliation can be tough before a couple has adequately resolved the more serious issues that led to their separation. These premature reconciliations are unwise because they are usually temporary and can actually hinder a healthier reconciliation or future restoration.

8. In your own broken relationship(s), do you think you should you seek restoration? If not now, what changes could make restoration possible in the future?

9. In your heart, what leads you to believe that restoration is possible for your relationship?

EMBRACING THE TRUTH – 25 MINUTES

LEADER: *This section addresses a variety of questions often asked regarding forgiveness.. Recite each of the questions that follow and invite the group members to share their answers. Make sure you affirm their responses. After members have sufficiently shared, present the answers offered below each question. This section should be a discussion that offers some researched solutions.*

1. How do you forgive someone who does not say he's sorry?

Jesus pronounced forgiveness from the cross in the very midst of His crucifixion. Many people that we will forgive will neither acknowledge any wrongdoing or even care that we have forgiven them. It's important to remember that we don't forgive because someone deserves, acknowledges, or even appreciates forgiveness. We forgive because it's so near to the heart of God, and because it's beneficial for us in bringing freedom into our lives.

2. How do you forgive someone when he or she continues to hurt you?

Forgiveness is challenging enough when you're dealing with past offenses, but sometimes the offenses don't stop. Divorced parents are a good example, with custody issues, visitation, and child support often causing the hurt to continue. This dynamic requires a special application of forgiveness, one that must be updated or occasionally upgraded like software. In such cases, reconciliation or restoration is not realistic or wise because the other person won't cease the damage. Romans 12:18 comes into play again because some people won't let you live at peace with them because they have no intention of living at peace with you. In situations like these, you must set boundaries and minimize contact.

3. Do you think it's necessary to tell the person you forgive her? Explain your thoughts.

Many people do not acknowledge that they've done anything wrong, so they don't have a real desire to be forgiven, and they will not thank you for your forgiveness. If you knew that someone would intentionally smash an expensive vase that you gave him or her as a gift, would you still offer the gift? Probably not. Don't tell someone you have forgiven them if the conversation is likely to provoke more conflict and bad feelings.

Forgiveness is a gift you can offer silently … that is as much of a gift for you as it is for them. And speaking of gifts, remember that you may still "gift" the offender in a thoughtful, tangible way without expecting a response and without announcing it as a token of forgiveness. Allow the "gifting" to communicate its implied message.

4. What if your attempts at reconciliation have setbacks?

Sometimes the old wound can be provoked by hearing a similar offense, meeting someone who reminds you of the offender, or even seeing a TV show or movie with a character or plot that's painfully familiar. It is important to remember that forgiveness is not forgetting. The anger is not immediately gone. It's relieved, and will continue to give way, but you can expect to have periods during which you find yourself struggling again. The key during these times is to avoid escalation, which leads back to bitterness and resentment—back at the beginning of the process as a prisoner of your own anger.

5. How do you forgive someone who is deceased?

Restoration with someone who's deceased is obviously not possible. Partial reconciliation is possible. A number of the exercises in this series apply to a damaged relationship with someone that has passed away. It is recommended that you engage in "The Eyes of Jesus" exercise as well as the forgiveness letter exercise with the deceased offender in mind. His or her death and absence should find its way into the content of those two exercises.

6. How do you forgive a person who hurt someone you love?

Sometimes the person we must forgive is someone who didn't hurt us directly, but injured a friend, spouse, or child. Remember that forgiving is not excusing or minimizing the wrong. Neither does forgiveness always include a reconciliation or restoration. Our forgiveness does not erase the pain our loved one feels. They must embark upon their own healing journey, and that can be agonizing to observe. Pray for your own healing and pray earnestly for the healing journey of your loved one.

LEADER: Close by asking for additional comments. If there are members who want to thank the group, or who would like to offer encouragement to the others, allow them time to do so.

CONNECTING – 20 MINUTES

SET FORGIVENESS FREE!

LEADER INSTRUCTIONS FOR THE GROUP EXPERIENCE: Give each person in the group one helium-filled balloons and a fine-point marker for writing on the balloon. If it's dark outside, step 1 will have to be done inside or around some outside light source.

Say to the group: "We discussed that forgiveness and reconciliation is a journey. Throughout our journey, we've discussed the importance of releasing our burdens to God.

STEP 1: Write the offender's name and list of offenses on the balloon with a permanent marker. Jot down brief phrases describing how you've felt. Lastly, write something like, "I choose to forgive you," or "I'm forgiving and healing," or "You are free so I am free."

STEP 2: In your time ... when you are ready to make a conscious decision to release those offenses ... open up your hand to release your balloon and give your burdens to God. He's been waiting for you to allow Him to carry you. Watch your balloon until you can no longer see it. This will remind you that you have released your burdens to God and they are no longer retrievable. Then, record in your journal what you felt as you released your balloon.

STEP 3: Talk with God and express your desire to release your hatred, freeing the prisoner and yourself as well. Listen for God to respond. Ask Him to give you one phrase or sentence of His delight in and plan for you."

1. What have been one or two of the most meaningful (encouraging, challenging, or helpful) ideas, principles, statements, or Scriptures you've encountered in this study?

2. What unanswered questions or unresolved issues do you still have?

3. How would you describe your progress along the healing Route to Reconciliation of forgiveness?

4. How has the group itself been particularly helpful to you?

MY PRAYER REQUESTS:

MY GROUP'S PRAYER REQUESTS:

LEADER PRAYER NOTE: Close by having people sit or stand in a circle, and join hands. As the leader, step behind each group member, and place your hands gently on his or her head or shoulders. Pray a brief personalized blessing over each group member in this way. Close with a prayerful benediction over the entire group as they continue to discover their freedom in Christ and move forward on the healing journey of forgiveness.

TAKING IT HOME

A QUESTION TO TAKE TO GOD:

When you ask God a question, expect His Spirit to respond to your heart and spirit. Be careful not to rush it or manufacture an answer. Don't write down what you think the "right answer" is. Don't turn the Bible into a reference book or spiritual encyclopedia. Just pose your question to God and wait for Him to speak personally in a fresh way. Be sure to write down what you hear or sense God saying to you.

✳ Jesus, in Galatians 5:1 we find that You set us free so we could stay free! Would You put a spotlight on those things in my life that are keeping me from freedom? How far do You want me to go with reconciliation and restoration in my broken relationship?

REQUIRED SUPPLIES AND PREPARATION FOR EACH SESSION

This section lists required supplies for Group Experiences in each session of the study.

SESSION 1:

Supplies: - If possible, a Swiss Army Knife or something similar as a visual aid while you're discussing this "Discovering the Truth" section
- A 4 x 6" index card or blank sheet of paper for each participant ...with pens

SESSION 2:

Supplies: - None required

SESSION 3:

Supplies: - Optional: CD *Pursued by God: Redemptive Worship Volume 1* from Serendipity House.

Preparation:

LISTENING PRAYER TIME:

You're going to lead group members in a short time of listening prayer.

SESSION 4:

Supplies: - Movie *Braveheart* on DVD
- TV/Screen and DVD system

Preparation:

Have a TV/DVD player set up close by, and the *Braveheart* movie cued up to the scene in which William Wallace (Mel Gibson) rips off the helmet of an enemy soldier, and discovers it's Isaac the Bruce, a fellow countryman, who has betrayed him. Show Scene 15 from 1:59:20 to 2:09:38 minutes on the DVD (begin at 2:05:00 if time is short).

SESSION 5:

Supplies: - CD *Pursued by God: Redemptive Worship Volume 1* from Serendipity House
- CD player or audio system

PERSONAL WRITING EXERCISE:

You're going to lead group members in a short personal writing exercise.

SESSION 6:

Supplies: - Movie *Les Misérables* (Liam Neeson, Geoffrey Rush) on DVD
- TV/Screen and DVD system

Preparation:

Have a TV/DVD player set up close by, and the *Les Miserables* (Liam Neeson, Geoffrey Rush) movie cued up to the scene in which Jean Valjean (Neeson) steals from the priest, gets captured and, is subsequently forgiven.

SESSION 7:

Supplies: - Copy of Lewis Smedes' book, *Forgive and Forget*
- Empty chair for each participant
- Ropes to drape over each empty chair
- Soft foam baseball bat or foam tube for each participant
- Movie *Legends of the Fall* (Liam Neeson, Geoffrey Rush) on DVD
- TV/Screen and DVD system

Preparation:

Locate a copy of Lewis Smedes' book *Forgive and Forget: Healing the Hurts We Don't Deserve* (San Francisco,: Harper, 1996).

"EYES OF JESUS" GROUP EXPERIENCE
It would be most effective to have ropes draped on an empty chair for each group member, as well as a soft foam baseball bat or foam tube.

LEGENDS OF THE FALL
There is a great scene from the film *Legends of the Fall* (Brad Pitt, Anthony Hopkins, Aiden Quinn) that serves as a dramatic illustration of the Prodigal Son story. Read the following paragraph, and then begin in Scene 24 (from 54:56 to 57:23 minutes on the DVD) as Tristan returns, riding back through the field to his home toward the reunion with his father. After viewing the scene, engage the group through the questions.

SESSION 8:

Supplies: - CD *Pursued by God: Redemptive Worship Volume 1* from Serendipity House
- CD player or audio system
- Helium-filled balloons on strings: At least one for each group member
- Fine-point markers: At least one for each group member

Preparation:

LEADER OPTION: A multi-dimensional worship and healing CD: *Pursued by God: Redemptive Worship Volume 1* is available from Serendipity House. As you begin this final session, you may want to play the song "All" and ask group members to listen.

Give each person in the group one helium-filled balloons and a fine-point marker for writing on the balloon. If it's dark outside, step 1 will have to be done inside or around some outside light source.

LEADING A SUCCESSFUL SUPPORT GROUP

You will find a great deal of helpful information in this section that will be crucial for success as you lead your group.

Reading through this and utilizing the suggested principles and practices will greatly enhance the group experience. You need to accept the limitations of leadership. You cannot transform a life. You must lead your group to the Bible, the Holy Spirit, and the power of Christian community. By doing so your group will have all the tools necessary to walk through the grieving process and embrace life and hope on the other side. The grief process normally lasts longer than eight weeks. But the connections that are built and the truths learned with allow your group members to move toward wholeness.

MAKE THE FOLLOWING THINGS AVAILABLE AT EACH SESSION

- *Radical Reconciliation* book for each attendee
- Bible for each attendee
- Boxes of tissue
- Snacks and refreshments
- Dark chocolates
- Pens or pencils for each attendee

THE SETTING

GENERAL TIPS:

1. Prepare for each meeting by reviewing the material, praying for each group member, asking the Holy Spirit to join you, and making Jesus the centerpiece of every experience.

2. Create the right environment by making sure chairs are arranged so each person can see the eyes of every other attendee. Set the room temperature at 69 degrees. If meeting in a home, make sure pets are in a location where they cannot interrupt the meeting. Request that cell phones are turned off unless someone is expecting an emergency call. Have music playing as people arrive (volume low enough for people to converse) and, if possible, burn a sweet-smelling candle.

3. Try to have soft drinks and coffee available for early arrivals.

4. Have someone with the spiritual gift of hospitality ready to make any new attendees feel welcome.

5. Be sure there is adequate lighting so that everyone can read without straining.

6. There are four types of questions used in each session: Observation (What is the passage telling us?), Interpretation (What does the passage mean?), Self-revelation (How am I doing in light of the truth unveiled?), and Application (Now that I know what I know, what will I do to integrate this truth into my life?). You won't be able to use all the questions in each study, but be sure to use some from each.

7. Connect with group members away from group time. The amount of participation you have during your group meetings is directly related to the amount of time you connect with your group members away from the meeting time.

8. Don't get impatient about the depth of relationship group members are experiencing. Building real Christian Community takes time.

9. Be sure pens and/or pencils are available for attendees at each meeting.

10. Never ask someone to pray aloud without first getting their permission.

Every Meeting:

1. Before the icebreakers, do not say, "Now we're going to do an icebreaker." The meeting should feel like a conversation from beginning to end, not a classroom experience.

2. Be certain every member responds to the icebreaker questions. The goal is for every person to hear his or her own voice early in the meeting. People will then feel comfortable to converse later on. If members can't think of a response, let them know you'll come back to them after the others have spoken.

3. Remember, a great group leader talks less than 10% of the time. If you ask a question and no one answers, just wait. If you create an environment where you fill the gaps of silence, the group will quickly learn they needn't join you in the conversation.

4. Don't be hesitant to call people by name as you ask them to respond to questions or to give their opinions. Be sensitive, but engage everyone in the conversation.

5. Don't ask people to read aloud unless you have gotten their permission prior to the meeting. Feel free to ask for volunteers to read.

THE GROUP

Each small group has it's own persona. Every group is made up of a unique set of personalities, backgrounds, and life experiences. This diversity creates a dynamic distinctive to that specific group of people. Embracing the unique character of your group and the individuals in that group is vital to group members experiencing all you're hoping for.

Treat each person as special, responsible, and valuable members of this Christian community. By doing so you'll bring out the best in each of them, thus creating a living, breathing, life-changing group dynamic.

WHAT CAN YOU EXPECT?

Because group members are still experiencing numbness and emotions are stirring within them, at the outset, members will be on their best behavior. Most attendees will, as they understand the openness necessary and requested by the group, withdrawal for a time.

Some attendees will experience fatigue which will lead to them shutting down emotionally. This is natural and is one of the things our body does to prevent emotional overload.

There are some emotions and phases unique to people dealing with struggles. You need to be aware of these.

Anger – normal, but maybe difficult to express due to shame or guilt. Clearly directed in the case of relational issues. Can be turned inward (depression).

Guilt – Sometimes called the "What ifs" or the "If onlys."

Sadness – This is generally in direct proportion to the attachment to the person or object lost. The greater the loss, the deeper the sadness.

Anxiety and Helplessness – Fear of the unknown can increase anxiety.

Frustration – Adjusting to the absence of things needed and cherished is normal. Becomes a problem when there are demands to go back to the way it was.

Depression – When the anger of a loss is directed inward

Loss of Identity – That which was lost is what gives some persons their sense of identity. Their self-worth is built around the job they used to have, the spouse they use to love and care for. When that thing no longer exists in their lives, they find themselves without and are lost in a sea of unknown meaning.

You will be the most helpful when you focus on how the each individual is adjusting and reminding them that these emotions are normal. When short tempers, changes in physical habits, such as sleep, eating, apathy, and others appear to be long term, refer them to a pastor or Christian counselor. You can get a list of counselors from your pastor and other ministers.

Places may also bring back memories that are difficult to deal with alone. If a member has an engagement in a location that would be a painful reminder of the past, go with them and/or ask the group if one of them might be there for this individual. You may hear, "This is something I have to do alone." You can respect their desire to be strong, but remind them that even alone, it is God who will give them strength, and that you will pray for them.

What Can You Do?

Support – Provide plenty of time for support among the group members. Encourage members to connect with each other between meetings when necessary.

Shared Feelings – Reassure the members how normal their feelings are—even if relief and sadness are mixed together. Encourage the members to share their feelings with one another.

Advice Giving – Avoid giving advice. Encourage cross-talk (members talking to each other), but limit advice giving. Should and ought to statements tend to increase the guilt the loss has already created.

Silence – Silence is not a problem. Even though it may seem awkward, silence is just a sign that people are not ready to talk. It DOES NOT mean they aren't thinking or feeling. If the silence needs to be broken, be sure you break it with the desire to move forward.

Prayer – Prayer is vital to healing. Starting and ending with prayer is important. However, people may need prayer in the middle of the session. Here's a way to know when the time is right to pray. If a member is sharing and you sense a need to pray, then begin to look for a place to add it.

Feelings vs. Right Choices and Thinking – There may be a temptation to overemphasize feelings rather that choices and thinking. It is important that you keep the focus on moving forward regardless of how we feel. Our feelings may make the journey slow, but left to feelings only, progress will shut down.

As you move toward the end of the study, be aware that it is a bittersweet time for the group. It will be painful for them to say goodbye to one another. Set a time for the group to have a reunion.

About the Writer

Ramon Presson, a clinically certified marriage and family therapist, has served as an assistant pastor and counselor for almost two decades. He is the founder of LifeChange Counseling and Coaching in Franklin, Tennessee.

Presson is the creator and co-author with Dr. Gary Chapman of both *Love Talks for Couples* and *Love Talks for Families*. He has also written three additional Serendipity House studies: *Vital Pursuits; Intentional Choices;* and *Radical Reconciliation.*

He has written articles for *Marriage Partnership, Discipleship Journal, Christian Single,* and is a frequent writer for *Single Adult Ministry Journal.*

Ramon lives with his wife and two sons in Thompson Station, Tennessee.

For more information about Ramon Presson or LifeChange, visit www.ramonpresson.com.

Acknowledgments

This project was a true team effort. We wish to thank the team that labored to make this life-changing small-group experience a reality.

Publisher: Ron Keck

Writer: Ramon Presson

Editorial team: Ben Colter, Brian Daniel, Lori Mayes, and Karen Daniel

Art direction: Brian Marschall

Cover and interior design: Roy Roper of WideyeDesign
Scott Lee of Scott Lee Designs

Welcome to Community!

MEETING TOGETHER WITH A GROUP OF PEOPLE TO STUDY GOD'S WORD AND EXPERIENCE LIFE TOGETHER IS AN EXCITING ADVENTURE.

A SMALL GROUP IS ... A GROUP OF PEOPLE UNWILLING TO SETTLE FOR ANYTHING LESS THAN REDEMPTIVE COMMUNITY.

Core Values

Community:

God is relational, so He created us to live in relationship with Him and one another. Authentic community involves sharing life together and connecting on many levels with the people in our group.

Group Process:

Developing authentic community requires a step-by-step process. It's a journey of sharing our stories with one another and learning together.

Stages of Development:

Every healthy group goes through various stages as it matures over a period of months or years. We begin with the birth of a new group, deepen our relationships in the growth and development stages, and ultimately multiply to form other new groups.

Interactive Bible Study:

God provided the Bible as an instruction manual of life. We need to deepen our understanding of God's Word. People learn and remember more as they wrestle with truth and learn from others. The process of Bible discovery and group interaction will enhance our growth.

EXPERIENTIAL GROWTH:

The goal of studying the Bible together is not merely a quest for knowledge, but should result in real life change. Beyond solely reading, studying, and dissecting the Bible, being a disciple of Christ involves reunifying knowledge with experience. We do this by bringing our questions to God, opening a dialogue with our hearts (instead of killing our desires), and utilizing other ways to listen to God speak to us (group interaction, nature, art, movies, circumstances, etc.). Experiential growth is always grounded in the Bible as God's primary means of revelation and our ultimate truth-source.

THE POWER OF GOD:

Our processes and strategies will be ineffective unless we invite and embrace the presence and power of God. In order to experience community and growth, Jesus needs to be the centerpiece of our group experiences and the Holy Spirit must be at work.

REDEMPTIVE COMMUNITY:

Healing occurs best within the context of community and relationships. A key aspect of our spiritual development and journey through grief and pain is seeing ourselves through the eyes of others, sharing our stories, and ultimately being set free from the secrets and lies we embrace that enslave our souls.

MISSION:

God has invited us into a larger story with a great mission. It is a mission that involves setting captives free and healing the broken-hearted (Isaiah 61:1-2). However, we can only join in this mission to the degree that we've let Jesus bind up our wounds and set us free. As a group experiences true redemptive community, other people will be attracted to that group, and through that group to Jesus. We should be alert to inviting others while we maintain (and continue to fill) an "empty chair" in our meetings to remind us of others who need to encounter God and authentic Christian community.

Sharing Your Stories

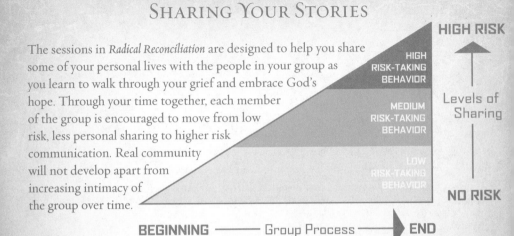

The sessions in *Radical Reconciliation* are designed to help you share some of your personal lives with the people in your group as you learn to walk through your grief and embrace God's hope. Through your time together, each member of the group is encouraged to move from low risk, less personal sharing to higher risk communication. Real community will not develop apart from increasing intimacy of the group over time.

HIGH RISK

HIGH RISK-TAKING BEHAVIOR

MEDIUM RISK-TAKING BEHAVIOR

Levels of Sharing

LOW RISK-TAKING BEHAVIOR

NO RISK

BEGINNING ——— Group Process ——▶ END

Sharing Your Lives

As you share your lives together during this time, it is important to recognize that it is God who has brought each person to this group, gifting the individuals to play a vital role in the group (1 Corinthians 12:11). Each of you was uniquely designed to contribute in your own unique way to building into the lives of the other people in your group. As you get to know one another better, consider the following four areas that will be unique for each person. These areas will help you get a "grip" how you can better support others and how they can support you.

G – SPIRITUAL GIFTS: God has given you unique spiritual gifts (1 Corinthians 12; Romans 12:3-8; Ephesians 4:1-16).

R – RESOURCES: You have resources that perhaps only you can share, including skill, abilities, possessions, money, and time (Acts 2:44-47; Ecclesiastes 4:9-12).

I – INDIVIDUAL: You have past experiences, both good and bad, that God can use to strengthen others (2 Corinthians 1:3-7; Romans 8:28).

P – PASSIONS: There are things that excite and motivate you. God has given you those desires and passions to use for His purposes (Psalm 37:4,23; Proverbs 3:5-6,13-18).

To better understand how a group should function and develop in these four areas, consider going through the Serendipity study entitled *Great Beginnings*.

Meeting Planner

The leader or facilitator of our group is _____ .
The apprentice facilitator for this group is _____ .

We will meet on the following dates and times:

	Date	Day	Time
Session 1			
Session 2			
Session 3			
Session 4			
Session 5			
Session 6			
Session 7			
Session 8			

We will meet at:

Session 1 _____
Session 2 _____
Session 3 _____
Session 4 _____
Session 5 _____
Session 6 _____
Session 7 _____
Session 8 _____

Refreshments will be arranged by:

Session 1 _____
Session 2 _____
Session 3 _____
Session 4 _____
Session 5 _____
Session 6 _____
Session 7 _____
Session 8 _____

Childcare will be arranged by:

Session 1 _____
Session 2 _____
Session 3 _____
Session 4 _____
Session 5 _____

Session 6 _____
Session 7 _____
Session 8 _____

GROUP DIRECTORY

Write your name on this page. Pass your books around, and ask your group members to fill in their names and contact information in each other's books.

Your Name: _____

Name: _____   Name: _____
Address: _____   Address: _____
City: _____   City: _____
Zip Code: _____   Zip Code: _____
Home Phone: _____   Home Phone: _____
Mobile Phone: _____   Mobile Phone: _____
E-mail: _____   E-mail: _____

Name: _____   Name: _____
Address: _____   Address: _____
City: _____   City: _____
Zip Code: _____   Zip Code: _____
Home Phone: _____   Home Phone: _____
Mobile Phone: _____   Mobile Phone: _____
E-mail: _____   E-mail: _____

Name: _____   Name: _____
Address: _____   Address: _____
City: _____   City: _____
Zip Code: _____   Zip Code: _____
Home Phone: _____   Home Phone: _____
Mobile Phone: _____   Mobile Phone: _____
E-mail: _____   E-mail: _____

Name: _____   Name: _____
Address: _____   Address: _____
City: _____   City: _____
Zip Code: _____   Zip Code: _____
Home Phone: _____   Home Phone: _____
Mobile Phone: _____   Mobile Phone: _____
E-mail: _____   E-mail: _____

Name: _____   Name: _____
Address: _____   Address: _____
City: _____   City: _____
Zip Code: _____   Zip Code: _____
Home Phone: _____   Home Phone: _____
Mobile Phone: _____   Mobile Phone: _____
E-mail: _____   E-mail: _____